TEACHING THE FAMILY

By the same author:

Teaching the Family

Edited by
MICHAEL BOTTING

CPAS

KINGSWAY PUBLICATIONS
EASTBOURNE

First published by Falcon Books 1973

This revised edition 1994

ISBN 0 86065 999 2

Published by Kingsway Publications in association with
the Church Pastoral Aid Society (CPAS), an Evangelical
Anglican organisation set up to support and help local
parishes in their work of mission. CPAS provides materials
and training for leaders of all age groups in the church
family, including clergy, housegroup leaders and those
involved in children's and youth work.
CPAS, Athena Drive, Tachbrook Park, Warwick CV34 6NG

Produced by Bookprint Creative Services
P.O. Box 827, BN23 6NX, England for
KINGSWAY PUBLICATIONS LTD
Lottbridge Drove, Eastbourne, E Sussex BN23 6NT.
Printed in England by Clays Ltd, St Ives plc

Contents

Foreword to First Edition
by the Bishop of Ely

Michael Botting has brought together in his new book his own deep concern for Bible teaching and study and an exceptional knowledge of modern audio and visual aids on the part of his contributors.

The church's teaching ministry requires a high degree of professional competence to keep pace with the rapid development of educational methods in other fields. *Teaching the Families* is not a technical handbook of religious teaching; yet its technique is modern, its ideas imaginative and its range is wide. But above all else it is the work of a group of men expressing their commitment to Christ by teaching the many families which together constitute that family of which Christ himself is the Head.

It is my belief that this book will bring new vision to those responsible for Christian teaching. It is my hope that it will be widely read, and then as widely used. Those responsible for its production will ask for no more than that.

✠ *Edward Elien*

Foreword to the Second Edition by the Most Revd Dr George Carey, Archbishop of Canterbury

The Decade of Evangelism provides a particularly good opportunity to reach those many in our country who are on the fringe of the church of Jesus Christ, and who need prayerful and loving encouragement to take the first step in.

I believe that Family Services, which have become such an exciting and prominent feature of our parochial life in the past twenty-five years, can help provide such a step.

For that reason it gives me very great pleasure to commend this revised and updated edition of *Teaching the Families*, which provides just the right basic biblical teaching that those on the fringe of the church require. Michael Botting and his contributors bring a high degree of imagination and professional competence to bear in presenting the Christian message in a way that is both memorable and challenging.

It is my prayer and hope that this revised book will bring new vision to another generation of those responsible for Christian teaching, as Bishop Edward Roberts believed it would for an earlier one.

✠ *George Cantuar*

Introduction

In the autumn of 1990 the Church Pastoral Aid Society organised a very successful tour to six centres in England during which various aspects of Sunday worship were dealt with in open sessions and in a choice of workshops. At five centres I led a workshop on preaching at Family Services. One fact that became abundantly clear to me was that curates and younger incumbents who attended my sessions, were totally unaware of my first book of talks *Teaching the Families*. I thought there might be a new market for it, and Kingsway agreed, asking me to revise and update the book.

With the co-operation of my original contributors the revision has now been completed and talks by some new contributors added. Most of the original talks have only undergone minimal changes, but the section on Audio and Visual Aids had become very out of date in some places and has been substantially altered, and all the material relating to drama and puppetry has been transferred to my book *Drama For All the Family*, also published by Kingsway.

The initial idea for this book arose out of a number of requests following the publication of my book *Reaching the Families* (now out of print) for a volume just concerned with Family Service talk outlines. As one correspondent wrote, 'I just have not the kind of mind that can produce these things.'

Objectives

Our combined writing has several objectives. Supporters of relief organisations like Oxfam and Christian Aid will know that their undertaking is not just to provide food for the starving, but also to help them to learn to grow their own so that they eventually become self-supporting. We hope that the talk outlines in this book will be a real help for those who have recently begun Family Services or are thinking of doing so, but we also hope the talks will help those responsible to train themselves in the art of speaking at Family Services.

Some of the outlines are deliberately extended to give assistance with the preparation of Family Service talks. Others are much more brief and you are left to fill in your own ideas and illustrations. Of course, for every talk you will need to pray to be guided by the Holy Spirit and fit it to the particular needs of your congregation. Anyone who believes it is only necessary to copy down the outlines and make a quick visual is doomed to immediate disappointment.

We would emphasise that the book is not intended to encourage laziness. The curate who regularly rushes in from the Saturday youth group and thinks he can just turn up one of these outlines has got his priorities wrong, though we all appreciate that there are occasional weeks in the rush and tumble of parish life when there *really* has not been a moment—in which case we hope some of these talks may be a useful last resort!

Every preacher, like every Christian, goes through dry patches, so we pray that for some these outlines may revive your vision.

Anyone who has been in the ministry for several years, especially in one place, tends to approach the major festivals with some foreboding. So in answer to a number of requests we are especially supplying several talks for Christmas, Good Friday, Easter and Harvest.

Basic assumptions

1. God's basic unit is the family, and the spiritual upbringing of children is clearly the responsibility of parents, not teachers or churches; though the latter can and should be a great help. God said concerning Abraham, 'I have chosen him, so that he will direct his children and his household after him to keep the way of the Lord by doing what is right and just, so that the Lord will bring about for Abraham what he has promised him' (Genesis 18:19). Moses told the children of Israel, 'These commandments that I give you today are to be upon your hearts. Impress them on your children. Talk about them when you sit at home and when you walk along the road, when you lie down and when you get up' (Deuteronomy 6:6,7). The Apostle Paul wrote to the Ephesians and other churches, 'Fathers, do not exasperate your children; instead, bring them up in the training and instruction of the Lord' (Ephesians 6:4).

2. The local church can and should help parents in their God-

given task, and the whole point of a Family Service is to do just this—in two ways.

(a) by providing a 'bridge' into the church for parents who previously have had little or no contact with Christianity;

(b) by providing a service in which parents and children can worship together.

The way in which the Family Service is designed to fulfil these aims will depend on many things—the type of area, the proximity of halls and other rooms to the church, the availability of teachers, and so on. It was gratifying to hear from one vicar who said his Family Service was founded very much on *Reaching the Families* lines: 'It has caused a revolution here! We have a full church every Sunday morning and have been able to get a curate on the strength of all the follow-up work that has resulted!'

More recently I heard of a vicar in a rural parish who inherited from his predecessor a very formal choir-dominated Eucharist attended by very few families. He eventually persuaded his church council to replace this at least once a month with a more informal Family Service. The vicar now has a different problem: not enough space in the church to seat all the families attending!

The point that needs to be made regarding the talks at Family Services is that in some churches parents and children will be sitting together throughout. In such cases care needs to be taken that all age groups are considered and that the service does not become just a children's service with adults present. In other churches on most Sundays of the month the children may go out for their own instruction in separate classes after the first fifteen or twenty minutes of the service. In which case a number of matters need to be borne in mind:

● Particular care should be taken with that opening quarter of an hour or so, that it is inspiring and intelligible for children as well as adults and that notices and banns of marriage are left until the children have withdrawn.

- If it is at all possible there is much to be said for having the early part of the service prepare both groups for the same lesson, and the going-home chat on the same teaching.
- The talk in church should still be reasonably simple and well illustrated, including the use of visual aids, such as an overhead projector. We live in the television age.
- Proper provision should be made during the Sunday for the spiritual nourishment of those who teach the children.

More For All the Family was published in November 1990. The *Church Times* kindly printed a review on 8th February 1991 by Dr Margaret Guite and I thank her for her very fair assessment. I very much hope that readers of the three books of talks I have edited will indeed use the ideas 'as a springboard for their own thinking'. By way of further explanation of the principles behind this book, I would like to comment on four other observations Dr Guite makes, which will necessitate my quoting parts of the review for the information of those who have not read it.

First she says that not all branches of the church can be summoned to give 'the kind of single-minded dedication to making an excellent and well-resourced presentation which characterises committed Evangelicals'. Surely with all the expertise, professionalism and resources that the world of commerce pours into advertising its transitory wares, Christian communicators should at least aim to present the eternal gospel unashamedly with similar dedication. Jesus challenges us, in his often misunderstood parable of the unjust steward, with the concluding words 'the people of this world are more shrewd in dealing with their own kind than are the people of light' (Luke 16:8b).

Secondly, Dr Guite says, 'I have no problem with the idea of preaching to convert, providing conversion is seen as a continuing process affecting every area of life, and provided family services do not aim simply to convince or teach, but also to catch the congregation up in worship.' As I say above I have always seen Family Services as primarily 'bridge' services to help the uncommitted into the worshipping and sacramental life of the church, so the 'preaching to convert' element is most emphatically intended to be present in most talks, though taken from a wide variety of approaches. However, if *Patterns for Worship* (CHP, 1989) is any guide, it speaks of Family Services 'reflecting an enormous amount of creative energy and the kind of God-centred worship that is resulting in a considerable growth of new Christians' (p 3). In *Liturgy for a New Century* edited by Michael Perham (SPCK/Alcuin Club 1991), Brian Spinks, in his chapter on Worship and Evangelism, acknowledges the value of Family Services as providing the 'bridge' which neither the 'quaint and archaic' BCP nor the 'middle-class' ASB do. However he rightly warns of the danger: 'Too many people seem content to attend the bridge service, and are content to remain on the bridge. They don't want to cross over to the main diet of worship' (pp 103-4). We who are parochial clergy must beware of resting on our laurels because we have a successful Family Service. Success can only be measured by the numbers of those who are actually moving on beyond the bridge.

Thirdly, Dr Guite writes that *More For All the Family* 'is very much a book of talks, and used alone could encourage the over-domination of the didactic element in a family service'. But if these services are for fringe members of the church surely they need Christian teaching, and where else will they get it? Part of the answer to the problem of moving people over the bridge lies in the nature of the talks given at Family Services, which the authors believe must be firmly based on biblical teaching, impart definite and clear Christian doctrine and cover the main part of the whole counsel of God. It is the word of God's grace, empowered by the Holy Spirit, that alone is able to build up and to give the inheritance among all those who are sanctified (see Acts 20:28).

Fourthly, Dr Guite will want to use the talks selectively

because she finds an over-emphasis on the threat of judgement in quite a few of the talks.

This theme is to be found in many of these talks simply because a gospel invitation is being offered. Jesus strongly implied that there are consequences if that invitation is refused. Obviously Jesus himself never spoke at Family Services as such, but the five great discourses that Matthew brings together in his gospel certainly had a considerable 'fringe' audience, and the theme of judgement is by no means absent (see Matthew 7:13, 21–23; 13:2, 30). I was very impressed by a comment made by the Archdeacon of Birmingham at the annual Diocesan Missioners' Conference in July 1991, that he aimed in his preaching to have something to say to those present for the first time and those there for the last.

The same features of my third book, which Dr Guite reviewed, are true of this revision of my first book, but the contributors hope and pray the positive side of the gospel shines through and will lead those 'fringe' members who attend our Family Services to a genuine commitment to Jesus Christ, and that they will grow up into mature and dedicated members of the family of God.

Peter Breckwoldt in his review of *More For All the Family* in the *Church of England Newspaper* of 15th March 1991 suggested that some indication of the length of talks should be given. I have to say that as these outlines are intended for people to build their own talks around, the length must be decided by them. Personally I aim to speak for not more than fifteen minutes at any Family Service.

Mr Breckwoldt also rightly implies that any ready-made resource needs to be adapted for local use, whether UPA, rural or suburban. In fact the authors of the talks in all my books come from a variety of areas including city-centres, but I hope no one will use our talks without adding both local and topical colour.

Acknowledgements

We all know how much we are indebted to others, particularly for secretarial help often freely given, or more recently to our word processors. I was, and still am, particularly grateful to the former occupant of the See of Ely, Bishop Edward Roberts, who provided the Foreword when the original book was published. Bishop Roberts, when Bishop of Kensington, gave me great encouragement to launch and persevere with the development of a Family Service at St Matthew's, Fulham in the early sixties when such a service was otherwise almost unheard of, especially in urban areas. I am extremely indebted to the Archbishop of Canterbury for writing the Foreword to this revised edition in the midst of an impossibly busy life.

Michael Botting
Chester, 1994

SECTION 1

Audio and Visual Aids

It seems to me vital that we should take considerable trouble to use good visual aids in our ministry—especially at Family Services. It is a very well established fact that people of all ages learn more from what they see than from what they hear. In a chapter on this subject in *Sunday School Teaching*,[1] Reginald Hill recounts the story of a teacher who was telling his Sunday school class about the healing of a leper, when it occurred to him to ask the boys, 'What is a leper?' He was shocked by the reply from one of them, 'Please, Sir, an animal with spots on'!

We live in an age when newspapers are struggling to keep going, and people of all ages spend an average of four and a half hours a day looking at 'the box'. Children are conditioned to learn in this way by the use of modern visual aids at school. I agree entirely with John Goldingay[2] when he writes that 'it is this declaring of the Truth that wins people, not the laying on of a Christian spectacular (whether in imitation of cults or of show business)'. Nevertheless visual aids, if good, create interest, dispel dullness, capture attention, give understanding, aid the memory and can thus convey and commend the gospel. Obviously Jesus used much simpler visual aids in his teaching, but life was so much less sophisticated in those days. Surely his message to us in our generation would be that we are to be even wiser than the children of darkness (Luke 16:8).

---

[1] Scripture Union, 1962

[2] Grove booklets on *Ministry and Worship*, No. 7, page 21

Some readers may be daunted by the cost of audio-visual equipment. However we need to bear in mind that for much too long the church has been associated by the outsider with the second-rate, the serious consequence being that the Christian message has been given a similar coding. People almost expect the church projector to fail. We should therefore take every reasonable precaution to make sure our audio-visual aids are efficient, and this may mean not using the cheapest equipment. How do we afford these items? I have reasoned this way: God expects us to be good stewards of the money he has committed to us. He expects us to set aside at least a tenth especially for his work. I suggest that we allocate part of that money to buying some good equipment and making sure it is kept in good order.

In this Section various people write from their own experience about the use of a wide variety of visual aid equipment.

Michael Botting
Editor

1

Verbal Aids

David Lewis writes here mainly from the point of view of children, but in a Family Service there may frequently be children of all ages—indeed when it comes to a good story do any of us ever grow up? Jesus said, 'Unless you turn and become like children, you will never enter the kingdom of heaven' (Matthew 18:3).

From Bangkok to Birmingham, from Sydney to Southend, every day thousands of children (and adults) sit down, are sat down, are tucked up, propped up and gathered around while someone tells a story. Still, from the bazaar in Fez to the classroom in South London and to the television set in suburbia, children will sit down and willingly listen to a story. More than that, they will clamour to hear a story well told. Those of us who have children have heard the cry so often, 'Please tell us a story.' Professionalism abounds on every hand and the Family Service preacher and Sunday school teacher can feel depressed by the polished performances of the trained day school teacher or the television presenter. Where do we start? Do we practise in front of a mirror or just pray that we will succeed?

It may sound contradictory from one who uses a great deal of visual aid in his ministry among children, but a story well told is still the best method of teaching children the truths of the Bible. It was our Lord's preferred method, and although he used visual aids like a coin, a fish, a few ears of corn, he still spent the greater part of his ministry just telling stories, to adults as well as children. We must remember that a child would sometimes rather visualise a situation and the characters himself. As a child I was often disappointed at seeing a film or pictures in a book after having read the story first with no visuals at all. They were not a bit like what I had imagined—my mental pictures were always so much better and more exciting.

It will be impossible in one short chapter to explain fully, let alone exhaust the subject of illustrations and story telling, especially in Christian work, but these few suggestions will place before the person who really wants to be the best for God, a plan to work from and a guide for a deeper study of the subject.

Simple rules to follow

1. Know your story thoroughly so that at no time during its telling do you have to hesitate for a word or a fact. You will lose the children completely if you cannot remember how many sons Noah had or how many stones were in David's sling.

2. Remember that to a great extent you will have to 'entertain' the children with the story. By that I mean that they will have to enjoy listening to it! If the children do not, then all your energy will be expended to no purpose at all. Yet entertainment must be skilfully used to present the truth you wish to get across or the meaning of the whole story. Otherwise all you have done is to keep the children happy for half an hour.

3. Before even starting to tell your story, fix firmly in your mind the one (and only one if possible) main truth or point, and emphasise that during the telling of the story. Too many ideas or truths will confuse the children. If I were

using the story of David and Goliath, then I would emphasise the fact that God was with David—all the time. That is perfectly sufficient; there is no need to draw meanings from every word or object. To me that is the glorious truth, that although he was just a boy and only a shepherd boy at that, God was with him, making him brave and giving him the victory over a huge man!

Do's and Don'ts

1. While always being very careful not to add to the Scriptures, it is always helpful for the children if you include in the stories as much background as possible. Use your powers of description: talk about the swaying palm trees and the hot, hot sun, the dusty roads and the smell of the pigs as they grunted around the prodigal son. It will add a great deal of interest and the children will 'see' the scene so much more closely.

2. Don't be afraid of letting yourself go and acting a bit as you tell your story! Enter into it, crouch up and peep furtively over your shoulder as Achan walks through the ruins of Jericho.

3. Do use your voice. This is probably your main vehicle for conveying the truth. Whisper secrets, bellow orders and speak in the first person singular if you can. Do not always say: 'And so and so said this and so and so said that'—it becomes awfully dry for the children to listen to. Rather, speak *for* David or any other person in the story. An example would be when the little boy brings his loaves and fishes to Jesus. Do not just say that he brought them and then leave it at that, but rather, 'The boy came to Jesus, looked up and just said, "Please Sir, I've not got very much but would you like to have these?"'

4. Do use your hands and don't stand stiffly to attention like a soldier. Let your hands become the sword that cuts off

Goliath's head. Actually pick up an invisible crown and crown Saul. Cover your ears with your hands when the walls of Jericho fall down and hide your arms so no one can see the leprosy when you talk about Naaman. This again is a matter of entering into the story and being involved with the characters.

5. Do watch your language and use words that children can understand and understand quickly. In a book children can go back over a difficult passage and re-read it. If the spoken word is lost to their ears it is lost for ever. Therefore speak distinctly, simply and plainly. It is much better to say 'cows in a field' than 'cattle in agricultural pasture'.

Sources of expertise

1. The children themselves. Observe them and study them; find out what makes them tick and what their interests are and use this knowledge in your illustrations and story telling.

2. Books *about* children for adults to read; books on understanding children and the way that they think. There are many about. They will give you an insight into the mind and behaviour of children.

3. Books written by experts *for* children. In other words, children's books and comics and anything else that comes your way. The whole range of the Puffin books would keep you busy for the next few years. Excellent stories about children in different times and situations and conditions. All will contribute something of value to the Christian worker, whether in style, language, use of words or a sense of what really interests children and what they read. Publishers will not print a book that will not sell and make them a profit. Even dear Enid Blyton, condemned on all sides by the educationalists, can teach us what interests a child.

4. Television programmes. The story telling is quite often (not always) brilliant on children's programmes. They are on at a difficult time of the day for most people to watch, but there will be the odd time when it is possible, or you might be able to video them. Notice the means of selling the story to the children and how the first few moments must capture their interest. If the child is not interested in the first minute of the story it will be very hard to recapture his mind later on.

Sources of stories

How often I have been asked where I find all the stories I use. To find suitable illustrations and stories is a full-time job and one may read three or four books before finding one suitable story. But it may help you to know the general sources where I get my stories.

1. The Bible, of course. Not all the stories are suitable for children, but there is a great library of them: stories of wars and bravery and adventure which cannot be equalled anywhere, and in which the truth about God and our Lord is so clear that all you need to do is just to tell the story simply.

2. Books. Remember that it is perfectly in order to use a secular theme or story to explain a biblical truth, as long as it is used only to explain the truth and does not become a substitute for the truth. Our Lord did this continually. To have a fund of stories at your finger tips you must read and read book after book, magazines and anything else you can find. Keep a file of newspaper cuttings or write out the stories in a book in rough outline. Never think that you will remember a particular story when you want it. Some years ago I read *God's Smuggler*.[1] and during the reading of it I

---

[1] Brother Andrew (Hodder & Stoughton, 1967)

noticed several excellent incidents that would make superb stories for use in my work. But I did not make a note of them, and today I cannot remember one of them or even what they were about. I know where to find them, of course, but the point is, I ought to have written them out and filed them.

3. Our own experience. Children simply love stories that we can preface with phrases like 'When I was a boy' or 'I had a granny who was seven foot tall' or 'At the end of my garden there's a horse that is very, very old'. By personally involving yourself with the story you seem to make it much more real to the child's experience. To the child who is scared of the dark a story that starts 'When I was little, there was an old brown dressing gown hanging behind my bedroom door and at night when it was dark, I used to think it was an old man hanging there just waiting to get me' will straight away warm his or her heart to the story teller, and a contact will be made and an understanding built up which is very precious.

4. Do not be afraid of making up your own stories. Invent situations and characters; there is nothing wrong with writing your own stories as long as the children are not led to understand that they are true. The Jungle Doctor Fables would be good examples.

There are countless children who are sitting comfortably just waiting for someone to begin! If you have never told a story to a group of children—off you go! 'Once upon a time' is as good a starter as ever it has been, but remember our stories are not about a person who once was, a long time ago, but about the One who was and is and will be.

David Lewis
Scripture Union staff

2
Visual Aids — General

The size of visual aids

Small groups, meeting in homes or minor halls, are well enough served by small visual aids.

However, it is no uncommon occurrence to see Christian speakers produce some almost undetectable object in a pulpit, causing grievous eyestrain in the back half of the church. Another phenomenon is the blackboard, placed for the convenience of the viewers on a tiny easel, with the result that no one behind the front row can see it without a periscope. Sometimes lettering is chosen on the assumption that church members bring binoculars.

Unless one has a small church, a realistic dimension for a visual aid board is about 5' by 4'. The lower edge should not be less than 48" from the ground, if the congregation is to have unimpeded visibility of the whole board.

Lettering should be at an absolute minimum of 2" (perhaps for sub-headings); in the main lettering it should be 3" or 4" in height (see separate section).

Outlining pictures

It is important to black-edge (or white) all pictures—boldly.
They look almost twice as effective.

The Esterbrook 'Flomaster' pen (felt-tip), which is refill-
able, is useful for this. Flake White Romney oil paint (or white
poster paint) is suitable for white edging.

For those who cannot draw

For those who cannot draw there are many mechanical aids to
get round this disability, from an inexpensive pantograph to
an epidiascope (compact models of which are available with
powerful quartz-iodine lamps, in contrast to the old ponderous
machines). These enable a person without any artistic skill to
'blow up' existing drawings (such as illustrations from Children's Bibles), a collection of which can be easily gathered
from innumerable sources to form part of a visual aid. Alternatively, the same end can be achieved by tracing an outline
on to an overhead projection transparency, and then projecting this on to card. Even if the original is not followed
slavishly, such mechanical helps do enable the person who
lacks all drawing skill to get proportions right.

If funds permit, computer-generated graphics and lettering
can be directly presented on projection screens via an overhead projector—a technique commonly used in commerce
and universities, but as yet rare in church contexts. It offers
great scope.

Michael Botting mentions the following in the appendix to
More For All the Family (Kingsway 1990) p.274:

> Computer-generated transparencies for OHPs can be made for
> those who have access to a graphics plotter or laser printer using
> the appropriate grade of film obtainable from Logos Graphics, 23
> Nottingham Road, Stapleford, Nottingham NG9 8AB (0602
> 391711). Clergy may find members of their congregation in indus-
> try who have such equipment available.

Note: Epidiascopes are not suitable for projecting material in halls and churches in, say, the way slide projectors or overhead projectors are. This is because there is so much light loss. Gnome or Braun make good models with a 5″ square picture acceptance; the very small ones, widely advertised in the national press 'small-ads', are too low-powered, and often will not accept larger images than about 2″ square.

Easels and stands

An adequate support for a 5′ by 4′ visual aid, to be used during a Family Service in a sizeable church building, will often have to be specially made.

It is an easy matter to scale up a normal (classroom) easel, and any handyman in the church fellowship can construct it. This can result in an inelegant structure, some 10′ high, but it will at least be effective. If a flanged arm, 12″ or 15″ long, is added, to swing over from the top (forwards), it will make the easel an effective support for a forward-leaning projection screen, as needed for the proper use of an overhead projector (i.e. an ordinary self-standing, forward-sloping screen). Such a jumbo-sized easel has many adaptations; if made from 2″ by 1″ it is not heavy.

Such an easel lends an added air of excitement to a talk, inasmuch as all but the tallest clergy need to scale a chair to reach the upper areas of the visual aid—which, amid flowing ecclesiastical robes, is attended by special perils, and can result in the total collapse of the structure. This can usually be got round with some quick aside.

Chartpak Rotex

Chartpak (among many other manufacturers) make an attractive aluminium easel, featuring a solid panel built-in blackboard (or whiteboard). It has telescopic legs, and can easily be adapted to the height needed for a church building. It features a rubber roller-clip at the top, which will hold securely many sheets of card, maps and so on. Other visual aid boards will stand securely on the easel, even one measuring 5' by 4'.

Rotating easels

A number of churches, faced with the problem of congregations that cannot see forward-facing visual aids, have devised stands that freely spin, permitting clear visibility to people in side-chapels, choirs and so on. These have to be specially made, but are well worth the effort.

At the church where I minister we use a double-sided 5' by 4' board, mounted on a heavy-duty mild-steel tripod, with a central column containing a ball-race at the top and bottom. A mild steel rod screws into the central column, and each of the two 5' by 4' boards are then mounted on this rotating rod, back-to-back, giving two picture surfaces 5' by 4' of dark blue nylon-velvet or 'Teazlegraph' material (see next section). The tripod was made for us by a small local engineering firm, to whom we explained our requirements.

Surfaces for visual aid boards

Flannelgraph

Too well known to require comment. It is very limited in the material it can support with reliability.

White formica

This is frequently used in schools now, instead of blackboard. One writes with a dry 'magic marker' instead of chalk, and the result is strikingly better. However, dry-based markers must be used, or else the formica will become stained—unless the wording is removed (with a damp cloth) within thirty minutes or so. It is a long task, with abrasive cleaning agents, to remove staining from spirit-markers.

Magnetic blackboards

These can be inexpensively made by gluing a sheet of thin-gauge steel on to plywood, and painting the steel with blackboard paint. (This should not be too thickly applied, or it dries with troublesome ridges.) Lettering, or pictures, can be placed with confidence on the surface using small pieces of magnetic strip (readily available).

Plastigraph

Plastigraph is (one) trade name for PVC with a shiny surface which clings to similar surfaces like a leech. It comes transparent or in a wide range of solid opaque colours.

A basic board can be covered with black Plastigraph; lettering, shapes, scenes, etc, can then be pressed on. There is no risk of them falling off, and the result is striking. However, the material is shiny, and can give problems by reflecting light in a troublesome way from certain angles.

Plastigraph has, in my view, far more valuable application in lettering (see below) than as a substitute for nylon velvet or flannelgraph.

Nylon velvet

This is a superlative visual aid surface used widely today on exhibition screens. In the earlier edition of this book it was also referred to by the trade name 'Teazlegraph', but E.J. Arnold and Sons of Leeds no longer produce it. The name, however, still appears in some of the talks in Section 2. The nylon velvet should be of a dark colour such as navy blue and is sometimes available with a foam-backing, which gives it extra durability.

Once a presentation board has been made (simply by gluing the fabric onto a sheet of 5′ by 4′ plywood, and adding a dowel frame) almost anything can be attached. Unlike Plastigraph, there are no glare problems; unlike flannelgraph, things do not fall off—even out of doors in a high wind! A single Velcro disc, quarter inch square, attached with Evostik (or Uhu glue) is said to be able to support a three-quarter pound weight. Several discs would enable one to put a 2lb box of chocolates on the board, should the occasion warrant it.

Principally, one can attach drawings cut from fluorescent or poster card. To the back must be stuck quarter-inch squares of Velcro, the nylon zip material obtainable from most big haberdashers. The squares should be attached sparingly, but the glue must be strong, such as Evostik or Uhu (which has an ideal nozzle for the job); otherwise it will be the glue that gives way, not the nylon hooks of the Velcro. Velcro can also be bought in bulk direct from the manufacturers. A self-adhesive 25 metre roll ($^7/_8''$ wide) of the 'hook' side is a good investment for churches with youth departments and Family Services. The manufacturer is SELECTUS Ltd, Biddulph, Stoke-on-Trent ST8 7RH (0782 522316).

(See also under Lettering for valuable applications of this material.)

Lettering

Good lettering is worth a lot of trouble when teaching with visual aids. Notice the trouble the advertising industry takes over style and lay-out.

Size of lettering

As a basic principle, 4″ lettering is to be aimed for. In smaller churches or halls one can get away with 2″ letters and figures, but not everyone may be as sharp-eyed as you from the back of the church!

Upper or lower case?

The quick answer is that younger children will be more likely to be capable of reading lower case (small letters) than upper (capitals).

Presentation of lettering

It is no small task to make up lettering using a stencil in the conventional way. Each letter must be positioned, pencilled in and filled in with a felt-tip pen. Mistakes are costly in terms of both time and materials.

An alternative method, made possible when using a nylon-velvet board, is to build up a stock of letters and numbers, each with a couple of Velcro discs on the back, cut from medium-weight (pulp-board) fluorescent card. Plastic lettering can be bought, but it is very expensive. A cheaper method is to photocopy enlarged letters of the alphabet to create your own stencils or templates.

Cover four strips of hardboard (6″ by 52″ for a 5′ by 4′ board) with nylon velvet of a constrasting colour to the presentation board; stretch the fabric tautly across the hardboard, and attach the overlap to the back with a hand stapler. Then put Velcro strips (three or four, each about 2″ long) on the back, also attached using a stapler.

You can now make up any lettering in next to no time from your stockpile, and put the whole word, or heading, on the board in one action. The same lettering can be used over and over again. Once the original stencil has been made, it is a matter of a once-for-all project to cut out the supply of lettering. Those skilled in the art of delegation may not even have to do it themselves at all! Indeed an elderly housebound Christian might be delighted to do it as a piece of service for the Lord.

A basic alphabet will obviously not require a uniform number of letters. A useful guide will be found in the following breakdown:

BASIC ALPHABET

A–18	J–9	S–20
B–12	K–8	T–20
C–12	L–12	U–15
D–12	M–9	V–7
E–20	N–12	W–9
F–10	O–14	X–3
G–10	P–10	Y–8
H–12	Q–4	Z–2
I–18	R–12	

Smaller off-cuts of hardboard, say 4″ by 25″, similarly covered in nylon velvet, are equally useful for sub-headings, single words and so on, using 2″ or 3″ lettering. Nylon velvet, often used for making curtains, can be bought at large fabric shops in a range of colours.

Once again, the same lettering can be used over and over again, as can the background heading boards.

It is worth making stencils from PVC rather than card, as they will not tear or crumple. They are easy to cut out (use a pair of sharp surgical scissors) and durable to keep.

Lettering made from card should be cut from pulp-board weight fluorescent card, which is strong but easy to cut; it is also much cheaper than the heavy board, which needs to be scored through with something of the order of a Stanley knife.

Fluorescent card in the pulp-board weight is now easy to obtain.

The best answer to one's own artistic limitations is to discover and harness the visual aid skills lurking in the congregation. Given notice, and some guidance, many talents are available to be used to great effect.

John Simons
Nailsea, Bristol

3

The Overhead Projector

The overhead projector (OHP) is a form of visual aid which, if properly used, gives no sense of being 'for the children'. Indeed, for many years it has been widely employed in adult courses in industry and army instruction centres. In much Family Service work we are in fact addressing the parents, allowing the children to listen in. We therefore welcome this machine as a most valuable reinforcement to our equipment.

Description

The commonest form is a box about 14″ square, with an opaque glass lid. The box contains a powerful electric light bulb, and a fan to keep things cool. A slender arm rises from one corner of the box holding a mirror and circular lens about 12″ above the glass lid. A picture or diagram drawn on a transparent sheet of plastic film, known as a transparency, is then laid on the glass top. The light passes through it, and the picture is directed by the mirror to a screen standing 3′ or 4′ *behind* the projector.

Important advantages

1. It may be used in full daylight. Sunlight falling on the screen is best avoided, but otherwise no drawing of curtains or blacking-out is required.
2. A brilliant, sharply defined picture 6' by 6' is easily obtained. For those called to work in monster Victorian churches it will be a relief to be able to produce pictures and diagrams clearly seen from those back pews so dearly loved by shortsighted (and deaf) members of the congregation!
3. The projector may be (and, I would add, should be) used unobtrusively. If used in church, it can be placed on the seat of a pew, and will not betray its presence apart from the arm which holds the lens. This is bound to protrude above the pew, and gives to an observant visitor the impression that a young cyclops has joined the congregation.

   In one church where I used to work there was a Victorian wrought-iron screen across the chancel arch, which my predecessor proposed to remove. Thereupon, 300 parishioners who rarely, if ever, attended worship, signed a petition and presented it to the Chancellor of the Diocese to say how much they valued it. So the poor vicar was thwarted. But, in retrospect, I am quite glad. I found it invaluable for hanging things on, and we fixed to it a roll-down overhead projection screen. Normally this was almost unnoticeable, but when it was needed, say for five minutes during a sermon, a sidesman was responsible for pulling it down. This was refreshingly different from a blacked-out church, with the main aisle blocked by a 2" by 2" projector and operator, and strewn with trip wires.

   In some churches there is no obvious way of erecting a screen, but see pages 44—46 for some suggestions.
4. The speaker faces the audience when operating the projector. He can therefore introduce his illustrative material with little interruption to what he is saying, and in some churches it is possible for the preacher to use the projector

without leaving the pulpit. Having said all this, perhaps I ought to add that (like other visual aids) an overhead projector must not be allowed to dominate worship. To feel that it must be used at every service would spell bondage. At times it should be put firmly away and be replaced by other forms of illustration.

Ways of using

Here are three possibilities, though no doubt there are many more. In giving a talk at the Family Service, it is useful:
1. *For gaining attention.* For example, your theme is 'loving one's neighbour'. After reading the text, you switch on one of Schultz's cartoon pictures, with Charlie Brown saying, 'I love the human race: it's people I can't stand.' The congregation laughs, the point is made and interest is aroused.
2. *For revision.* If, when reading, we lose the thread of the argument, we can always stop, go back, and re-read. In listening to a talk, no such course of action is open to us, and therefore it is wise for a speaker to stop from time to time and to say in effect, 'For the sake of those who are lost, or who have fallen asleep, you can now see on the screen where we are, and the points we have already covered.'
3. *For clarification.* Some years ago I attended an army course on what, if anything, could be done in the event of a nuclear attack on this country. Probably all of those present possessed a university degree, and yet whenever there was anything which could conceivably have confused our simple minds a diagram was thrown on the screen by an overhead projector. This was good teaching. We often find ourselves addressing congregations less highly educated, and in trying to teach difficult doctrines or to expound hard passages, we should not neglect the use of suitable diagrams and pictures. I remember once attempting to expound Revelation 12—a rash task you might think. But I was able to flash on the overhead projector screen a most

intimidating and redoubtable red dragon with seven heads and ten horns, which had been superbly drawn for me by a friend, and we never looked back! Incidentally, television has so raised the standards of the viewer that no visual aid is better than a poor, amateurish drawing.

This leads me on to two final questions. First, if you have no artistic ability, who will produce pictures for you? There may well be someone in your congregation who would be willing to help. However, remember that this may cost him or her a lot in time and hard work, and so briefing may need to take place well ahead. One word of warning: much contemporary art is satirical, with ugly faces and figures. These should be avoided. The line drawings in *Punch* in the fifties and sixties are the ideal model—simple, full of fun, and, incidentally, very skilled. These and similar drawings can often be cut out, filed away, and then traced when needed.

Secondly, how much will an overhead projector cost? Prices vary quite considerably, starting (at 1994 prices) from £210 (plus VAT) and moving up to £400 or £500 or more. Readers are strongly advised to visit an audio-visual centre, so that they can choose the equipment which is most suitable for their requirements. Yellow Pages may be a help here. Also, I recommend a twin lamp model. This means that if a bulb expires in the middle of a talk, the touch of a switch avoids disaster. Also, a portable overhead projector, though more expensive, has great attractions for a parish where there are likely to be frequent moves between worship centres. The cost of a screen (which must have an extension bracket to enable it to be tilted forward to avoid a keystone effect), plus pencils and transparencies, will add at least another £100 to the initial bill. One should bear in mind that cheap equipment which constantly requires the replacement of bulbs will soon prove a bad investment.

For many parishes £400 or so may seem a lot of money, but I believe that where there's a will there's a way, and I agree with Michael Botting's comments on page 23 concerning purchasing one's own machine, if need be by tithing.

In building up the life of a parish, we need good, contemporary equipment, and we need it at once, not in ten years' time after the spire has been repaired and the chancel has been redecorated, etc. Once the overhead projector is in place, and being skilfully used, most members of the Parochial Church Council will soon be persuaded of its unique value.

John T. C. B. Collins
Retired, Lymington

Editor's note

The Sales Manager of Fisher Audio-Visual, Mr Charles Woods, 267-9 Old Chester Road, Birkenhead, Merseyside (051 644 8585), who supply throughout Britain, says that their middle range twin-lamped projector Kindermann Novascope costs £435, but his firm would be willing to supply machines at £299 plus carriage, if applicable, plus VAT. Bulbs (A1/233) cost £5 each. Further information can be obtained by writing or phoning for Fisher's comprehensive catalogue.

John Anscombe has contributed a chapter on overhead projectors in my book *For All the Family* (Kingsway, 1984), though obviously the prices he mentions will be out of date. There is also some more recent information in my book *More For All the Family* (Kingsway, 1990) pp 273-5.

4

Sound-strips

Here we are concerned mainly with film-strips and accompanying tape or cassette recorded sound. Films can also be shown in church using a daylight screen by having a mirror behind the screen at an angle of 45 degrees and projecting at right angles onto the mirror. This enables the picture, and in particular any words, on the film to appear the correct way

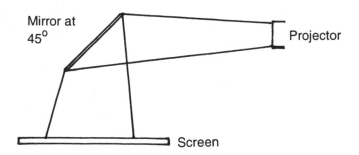

round. However the number of films suitable for Family Services is limited and the sound in churches can often be difficult to hear. There are a lot of suitable videos that can be used and John Anscombe provides a chapter in my book *More For All the Family* (Kingsway, 1990) on Using Videos with Large Groups.

Projectors

There is a wide range of film-strip projectors available. If your church does not possess one you may be able to borrow one from your local school, who are not likely to be using it on Sunday, though you may have to collect it late on Friday afternoon and promise faithfully to return it first thing on Monday morning. The main factor is to make sure that the lens is such that you can reasonably fill your daylight screen without being too far away, which would cause the picture to be too dim. You may find that if the projector is placed on the Communion Table the throw is just about right. I have done this, covering it with a white cloth during the earlier part of the service before the projector is needed, and removing it totally afterwards. I have never had any objection to this practice.

Daylight screens

Daylight translucent screen material for back-projection of film-strips or OHP transparencies can be set up in church but requires a certain amount of sanctified imagination. I will describe what I have done in two very different churches.

I have two 2″ by 2″ posts 10′ tall which drop snugly into steel brackets which have been screwed to the ends of the choirstalls facing the nave. The brackets have been made out of some strips of steel which can be fairly easily bent. Near the top of these posts are two strong metal eyes through which have been threaded strong nylon rope. On one end of each of these ropes are dog-clips. These fit onto metal eyes at each end of a beam that carries the daylight screen material. The very weight of this beam encourages the dog-clips to remain closed. The beam is a circular piece of wood about 1¹/₄″ diameter, and just an inch or two longer than the distance between the two upright posts. Onto this beam is fixed strongly with fish glue (or Bostick) and drawing pins the daylight screen material. Because the church was large I used two widths of material side by side and joined them down the middle on both sides with 1″ wide sellotape. A piece of dowelling was then fitted over the drawing pins and nailed down. On the other end of the material there is a similar, but shorter, beam to which it is fixed in the same way as on the upper one.

The ropes on the upper beam can both be pulled up and fastened to two open hooks on the upright posts.

Slightly thinner nylon rope is attached firmly at each end of the lower beam. This rope rises vertically on both sides of the screen and passes through eyelets screwed onto the upper beam. The rope from one end of the upper beam then comes horizontally along it and through the other eyelet at the other end of the beam. The ropes can then be pulled at the same time as illustrated.

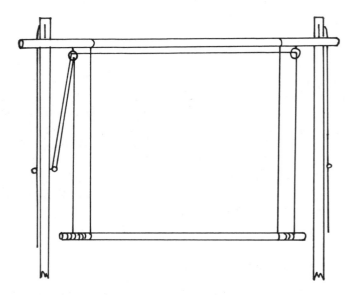

The ropes are wound round the protruding ends of the lower beam in such a way that when the beam is down, ie unrolled, the rope is rolled round the lower beam ends. When the ropes are pulled together the screen rolls up. An additional

46

hook is placed on one of the uprights round which the nylon rope can be wound when the screen is not required. The advantage of this arrangement is that the whole screen, which can be erected in three or four minutes, can be raised or lowered during the service in a matter of seconds. All the woodwork used in the construction is painted black.

In another church I had a beam as long as the chancel arch. Behind the arches on either side of the chancel were two short chains attached to the stonework. At the ends of the chains were dog-clips which engaged with strong metal eyes near the ends of the beam. The screen was similar to the one above in the way it rolled up, but the top of it had metal eyes that fixed onto open hooks on the beam. The beam was erected high enough for everyone in the church to see easily, but low enough for the whole apparatus to be reasonably easily fixed, requiring no more than a chair to stand on to reach the dog-clips at the ends of the chains.

Amplification

Regarding sound production, many churches today have amplification systems with facilities for playing cassettes. If such is not available, a good quality cassette player can be adequate in smaller churches. Failing that a cassette player can be connected up with appropriate leads to a good quality tape recorder, which thus becomes an amplifier. If that proves inadequate, loud-speakers can often be fitted to the tape recorder.

Film-strips and sound-strips

More and more organisations that produce film-strips are also making tape or cassette recorded commentaries to accompany them. Such organisations are usually prepared to hire their products, but they will rarely hire tapes because these are so easily damaged. It is my personal opinion that if a sound-strip is worth using at all it is well worth purchasing, as the hire price is often only one-sixth of the total cost.

If there is no tape-recording to accompany a strip it is not very difficult to prepare your own, and this is strongly recommended as it enables other voices to be used, sound effects to be employed and background music to be added, perhaps by your church organist or a music group.

The film-strips must be selected carefully, for we should never use one we have not previously examined to make sure it really does deal with the story as we should wish. The following are suggested sources for supply:

Bible Society, Stonehill Green, Westlea, Swindon SN5 7DG (0793 513713).

Church Army Resource Centre, Independence Road, London SE3 9LG (081-318 1226).

Church Pastoral Aid Society, Athena Drive, Tachbrook Park, Warwick CV34 6NG (0926 334242).

Concordia Publishing House, 28 Huntingdon Road, Cambridge CB3 0HH (0223 65113).

Scripture Union (for hire of videos and sound-strips), 9-11 Clothier Road, Brislington, Bristol BS4 5RL (0272 771131); (for purchase of videos, sound-strips and sound cassettes) PO Box 38, Bristol BS99 7NA. Write for catalogue.

SPCK, Holy Trinity Church, Marylebone Road, London NW1 (071-387 5282).

Bible News Ltd, Holland House, 39-40 Hythe Road, London NW10 6UN, publish on cassettes news broadcasts of biblical events in the idiom of modern news reporting. There are five cassettes covering ten programmes in each series: *Abraham to King Saul* and *The Jesus Programme*.

When using the sound-strip by back projection the strip itself has not only to be fixed into the projector upside-down but also back-to-front.

So many sound-strips produced these days, such as those from Scripture Union, tell Bible stories graphically, such as

48

the story of David, some major stories from the gospels and the Acts of the Apostles. They can be used in place of the Lesson, and from my personal experience will be much better remembered. It is important, however, to make sure that everything is carefully planned for when the sound-strip is to be used. My practice is for the sound and strip to be exactly ready, the projector focused and someone, possibly a verger or church warden in the congregation, to operate the church lights if necessary. I make sure there is some singing either side of the sound-strip during which the screen is lowered or raised and the projector uncovered or removed. If there are some more traditional members of the church who are not too sure about the use of these modern ways of proclaiming Christian truth, they are less likely to complain if the whole operation goes without a hitch.

Michael Botting
Editor

5

Congregational Participation

Giving an address should be a two-way communication, from the preacher to his audience and in response from the audience to the preacher. Try then to bring your congregation into it by actually using them in the talk. Sometimes, of course, they should also take part in the service by saying prayers with you, by singing the hymns and reading the lessons. But in the talk they should identify themselves with the message the preacher gives. There are various methods of helping them to do this. You can use one of them as an illustration: 'Now you see Mr Smith there, he is a builder and can tell you about the need for having a good foundation for a house. We also need a good foundation for our lives.' Only make sure that Mr Smith *is* a builder and does not mind being singled out in that way. Grown-ups are usually more bashful than children and some prefer to remain unidentified. Sometimes even missionaries and their families prefer not to be put in the limelight when they are on holiday at home.

By bringing the congregation into your talk you will help them to remember the message. Consider how you yourself react when someone at a meeting makes reference to you or points you out. It has the effect of making you sit up and take notice. You will go away remembering the part which included yourself if nothing else. It turns eyes onto you and causes interest for those listening. It is, though, very important that this kind of special attention is not abused and is only used when appropriate.

If you ask children to repeat a text, this helps them to remember the words. It also makes them part of the address. You must ensure, though, that the repetition is not a dull drone like a lot of children repeating the twice-times table, but is done in a way that excites their interest and where there is a desire to join in. Participation should always be willing and enjoyable, not a kind of conscription to save the speaker from disaster. On the whole adults are less willing to be made part of the talk than children, who mostly love to be asked unless they are very shy. Here are some of the ways of bringing them into the talk.

You can ask a general question to evoke a response: say, for example, 'Hands up everyone who came to church by car.' In this modern age that question will evoke a lot of hands. Be sure that your question is going to get the response you want or you may get off to a bad start, like the writer who took a toy helicopter to church which was powered by elastic, and in trying to get from the children that the power in the helicopter was the elastic and the power in our lives is the Holy Spirit, was told by a bright child that he was illustrating the Ascension!

You can make the illustration personal to the child: 'Suppose Jeremy there had a row with John (sitting next to him) like Paul had with Mark...' It helps to bring the story home and will probably cause everyone to look at Jeremy and John as you say it. They become part of your talk.

Then children will do things you tell them to, providing it is not too difficult. You want to illustrate 'a still small voice'. Get them to shut their eyes and listen hard to a whisper. The same can be done to explain blindness—get them to put their hands over their eyes.

Children often enjoy being up the front on the platform with the speaker. You can get them to hold up or build up

your visual aid. Some of the talks in this book can be so organised that the children hold the visual aid.

You can also arrange your talk so as to complete a crossword puzzle. To do this you divide the congregation into two halves ('across' and 'down'). The 'across' side has to answer the clues you give for the 'across' clues and the 'down' side answers the 'down' clues. This method is all right providing you know how to make a crossword puzzle and have the time and energy to do it. A simpler variation to this is to divide the congregation into two halves and run a noughts-and-crosses quiz on the talk as you go along, choosing a child from each side to place the 'O' and the 'X' in the squares which you draw or cut out in cardboard and place on a board. It is not a good idea to do this too often because the congregation does not attend a service to play party games but to learn and to worship and to hear. They will tire of continuous crosswords or noughts and crosses, but for an occasional talk it will add variety and involve the congregation.

Children can be used in the talk by teaching them to mime the persons you are talking about. For example, you want to give an address on a man who was deaf and dumb. You teach a child to behave deaf and dumb beside you as you talk to him. I once hand-cuffed the curate to illustrate 'captivity' in a talk about the children of Israel in bondage in Egypt. It had been intended to handcuff children but their wrists were too small. Unfortunately the curate's were large and it was not the easiest of tasks to release him to complete the service! Such details have to be considered when you use your congregation to participate in the talk.

Children too have to be used with due regard to their capabilities. If you use them to hold up a picture or words or cards in front of the congregation, make sure that your child is not too small and the visual aid too large, and the length of time they have to hold it is not too long. You may have a problem on your hands if you fail to do this. You invite someone to come up from the back and then find out that he or she is walking in plaster or with crutches. This has happened and creates a problem which needs a bit of quick thinking—be ready for it! Above all do not embarrass anyone who comes to help you or they will never come again. This means that you do not continually ask questions of children which are too difficult to answer or build visual aids which are beyond their capabilities.

Children love the chance to join in shouting when their minds are absorbed with what they are to shout, and if this is done on the right occasion you can bring your talk alive with a shout of response. You have probably seen this done at a pantomime or sketch performed to amuse children where, for example, the children are shouting 'look out' as the villain goes behind the hero to kill him, or where they are invited to shout a word of warning every time the villain appears on the stage. Of course the children have to be absorbed with what is going on in front of them for this to be effective, so you will not bring alive a boring address by a response the children are not interested to make. How do you do this effectively? Here is an example: Write on a card in large letters the words you want them to shout: 'Thank you.' Then you give a talk on saying 'Thank you' to God for his good gifts (at harvest time perhaps). During the talk you ask: 'What do we say to God?' and you hold up the card and as you do so the children shout 'Thank you' back again.

The use of mime is another method of making the congregation participate in the talk. Mime is enacting a story or a situation in front of the congregation without a word being spoken by the actors, and it is all done by gestures and movements. The person giving the talk can speak and tell the story from the pulpit while the actors from the congregation take part in the mime in front of him or to the side of him. For this you can use children or adults. You can also use a tape-recorded background of music or you can arrange the whole commentary and music on tape like a BBC documentary programme. The mime does not have to last the whole sermon time; it need only be short and part of the talk, simply illustrating a point you wish to make.

With all these methods of bringing the congregation into the talk, the primary object is to capture their minds with the truth you are seeking to explain from the Bible and to make that truth come alive to them. They are not just gimmicks to get attention, nor novelties for their own sake. You will no doubt discover that some of these methods suit you and others do not, according to your capabilities and the type of congregation you have. It is obviously no use asking elderly ladies to shout 'Thank you', or asking three-year-old children to do crossword puzzles.

In conclusion it is perhaps appropriate to mention here one further way in which adults particularly may participate in your talks. They may have no gift for speaking, but perhaps they can draw or do lettering and will be glad to share in making splendid visual aids, for which you may have no talent and very limited time.

Christopher Porteous
Beckenham

6

Filing Visual Aids

Sooner or later a Family Service preacher is going to have a filing problem, unless he throws away his pictures or transparencies once used (not to be recommended). So, how are they to be stored?

Try to use the same size card/paper every time (or double, and folded to file). A1 or A2 are pretty standard sizes, and easily obtainable. Filing vertically is easier than filing horizontally and the space between a filing cabinet and the wall is elastic—moving the cabinet further away from the wall as your stock of pictures grows.

You will need some form of simple container. A4 acetates are easy to store in A4 folders, but for paper sheets I find corrugated cardboard is the cheapest and easiest. Cut a piece from a large carton (electricity showrooms or radio shops can help) about 24″ by 72″ and fold as shown (Figure 1). This will take comfortably up to 70 sheets of papers. When closed you can slide this in and out of the filing space quite easily.

Number your visual aids—each sheet used in one talk having the same number; extra sheets, eg backgrounds (hills, villages, night sky, seascape, etc), illustrations (footballers, swimmer, family, office, house, etc) numbered individually or in groups (Eastern house, modern house, house with garage, interior of house could all have the same number).

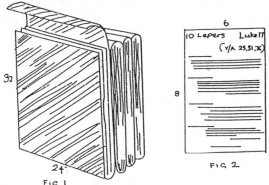

32

24

FIG 1

6

10 Lepers   Luke 17
     (v/a 25,31,76)

8

FIG 2

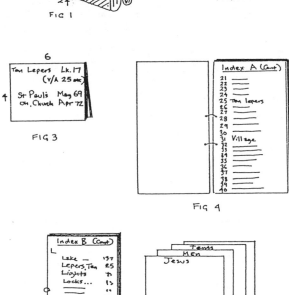

6

Ten Lepers   Lk. 17
      (v/a 25 etc)

4   St Pauls   May 69
     Ch. Church Apr 72

FIG 3

Index A (Cont)

21
22
23
24
25 Ten lepers
26
27
28
29
30
31 Village
32
33
34
35
36
37
38
39
40

FIG 4

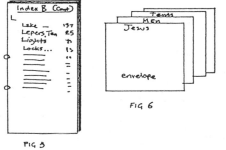

Index B (Cont)

L
     Lake —   137
     Lepers, Ten   25
     Lights   71
     Locks...   13

FIG 5

Tents

Men

Jesus

envelope

FIG 6

Your notes will be filed in a drawer or envelope with the number of visual aids used written at the top (Figure 2). Using paper for your notes twice the size of your filing card drawer is useful, because then you can fold it in two and it does not need stapling (staples go rusty!) and you can write the text/topic at the top and the date and place used in the middle (Figure 3).

Your pictures should be indexed on two lists. A4 sheets are adequate, but more sophisticated systems could be developed. Index A is a list of pictures in numerical order (Figure 4), and Index B is a list of pictures on alphabetical sheets (Figure 5).

Another useful file is a drawer of large envelopes for oddments (Figure 6)—save your large envelopes and put in them pictures of men, of a Bible, of animals, tents and so on.

Also if you want to keep flash cards, or the wording used on visual aids, which would otherwise get lost in the big paper files, put these in envelopes too and file them in alphabetical or biblical order.

If you use masking tape folded over, double-sided sellotape or blutak, remember to remove these pieces from the pictures before filing.

Peter Barton
Malmesbury

SECTION 2
Outline Talks

The Christian Year

1 Advent

TEXTS

Matthew 25:1–13; John 1:11.

AIM

To show that we must prepare for the coming of Jesus (i) at Christmas, (ii) into our lives day by day and (iii) when he comes finally in glory.

PRESENTATION

Point of contact:

Have you ever been to a wedding? Talk about the preparations made (perhaps show veil, buttonhole carnation, ring). Explain weddings in Jesus' time were different in some respects—at night—bridesmaids' procession would go to meet groom and his friends—return to bride's home. They needed lamps (show picture of lamp, or actual modern equivalent, and explain how ample oil was necessary).

1. Tell parable

Stress preparations bridesmaids would have made. Five sensible ones took thought, time and trouble to prepare lamps properly. Five foolish didn't—wonder why? (Pose

question at this point, without attempting to answer.)
Bridesmaids went to meet bridegroom—fell asleep while
waiting—awakened. Foolish found lamps gone out—went
for oil—missed the wedding.

2. *Examine reasons*

...why foolish failed to prepare lamps properly. Have simple outline sketches of the five girls, each giving her
reason—in 'balloon' from mouth.

1st: 'I was too busy.'

2nd: 'It was too much trouble.'

3rd: 'I forgot—I didn't think.'

4th: 'I thought my friends would lend me some oil.'

5th: 'I copied the others.'

Do you sometimes make excuses like these when things go
wrong? In the bridesmaids' case, it had very sad consequences.

3. *Share sad comment*

...made on Jesus' coming to this world—John 1:11 (read).
Imagine knocking at your own front door and being turned
away! Why did Jesus' own people miss him when he came?
Was it for the same reasons as foolish bridesmaids? Were
they too busy—preoccupied—thoughtless—careless—
influenced by others? (Elaborate on any of these as appropriate.)

4. *Look forward*

...to celebrating the coming of Jesus. We do this on December 25th. But he is always coming to us—asking us to
follow him, to love him, to serve him. Are *we* too busy, too
thoughtless, too ready to listen to friends—to be ready for
him? If so, we shall be unhappy when we realise, perhaps
too late, that we have missed him—because he is definitely
coming! Go on to stress his promised return.

5. Jesus has promised

...that, one day, he will come again. Do we ever think about that? The way we can prepare for that is by getting to *know* him, loving and serving him here and now. In that way alone can we be sure to be ready when he comes.

Conclusion

As we are involved with all the preparations for Christmas, focus attention on our need *to be ready* by revealing things which illustrate people's preparations for the Festival. Let us not miss the most vital one—preparing for Jesus. Then we shall be ready, not only to celebrate Christmas in the best way, but also to welcome Jesus when he finally returns, as he has promised. *Our* lamps will be burning brightly.

Garth Grinham
Southport

2   The Clock—an Advent Address

TEXT

Ecclesiastes 3:1–8.

AIM

To teach that God is the Lord of time and that he controls it.

PREPARATION

Make a grandfather clock out of two pieces of cardboard, as shown. On one piece draw the outline of a clock; the face has a hole in the top of it through which the words are to appear. Write 'Dec 25th', 'Every day' and 'Now' on a round piece of cardboard the same shape as the clock face, so that when it is turned round the words appear in the window. Attach the round piece of card behind the clock by a split-pin, and the hands in front. On the second piece of cardboard, write behind the door of the clock the text 'My times are in your hands', and fix the door in place with a split-pin or paper clip.

PRESENTATION

Introduction

Show how our lives are governed by time, e.g. time to go to school, time to get up, time for my birthday, and point out that

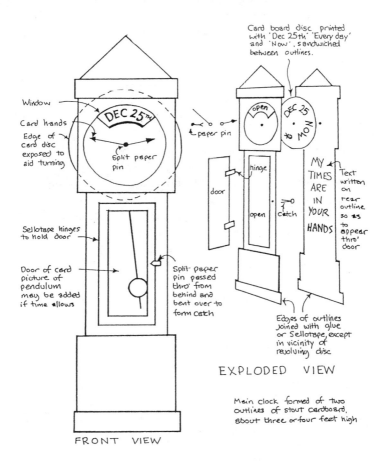

Card board disc printed with 'Dec 25th' 'Every day' and 'Now', sandwiched between outlines.

Window

Card hands

Edge of card disc exposed to aid turning

DEC 25th

Split paper pin

Sellotape hinges to hold door

Door of card picture of pendulum may be added if time allows

Split paper pin passed thro' from behind and bent over to form catch

FRONT VIEW

paper pin

open

DEC 25 MON

hinge

door

open

catch

MY TIMES ARE IN YOUR HANDS

Text written on rear outline so as to appear thro' door

Edges of outlines joined with glue or Sellotape, except in vicinity of revolving disc

EXPLODED VIEW

Main clock formed of two outlines of stout cardboard, about three or four feet high time always goes forwards, even when the clock stops. It is important to know the right time to do something otherwise you may miss it, e.g. your bus, the television programme or even Sunday school! God is Lord of time.

December 25th

Produce the clock and say that this clock shows 'God's time' (putting December 25th on the clock). Ask what the time was on December 25th when the star appeared. The answer is in Ecclesiastes 3:2: 'a time to be born'. Point out that in the Bible we are told that Jesus was born 'in the fulness of time'. The world had had Greek philosophy, Roman civilisation and Jewish religion—yet none of these were able to solve the problem of man's nature. God then sent his Son. In the same way as there was a time for Jesus to be born, so there will be a time for him to come again. We do not know the time but God does (Acts 1:7). It will happen in God's good time.

Every day

Put 'every day' on to the clock and ask 'What is the time every day?' You may get all kinds of answers to this. The answer you want is in Ecclesiastes 3:8: 'A time to love'. Point out that every day, every moment of our lives God loves us. He did in the past by sending his Son, he does now because Jesus promised he would never leave us nor forsake us: 'Lo, I am with you always, to the close of the age.' Show how when others do not love us, God does. God loves us all the time, just as good parents love their children all the time.

Now

Lastly, turn the clock face to show 'now', and ask 'What is the time now?' Make sure you know the answer—some child will tell you from his watch. The answer you want is 'a time to seek' (Ecclesiastes 3:6). Show them how Jesus was always seeking those whom he loved. Tell of the lost coin and the lost sheep—they had to be found. Jesus said he came to seek and to save that which was lost. The time Jesus wants us is now: delay is dangerous. '*Now* is the acceptable time; *now* is the day of salvation,' says Paul (2 Corinthians 6:2). Also point out the warning in Hebrews 2:3 that we should believe today, now, before it is too late.

Conclusion

For the Christian, God's time is always right and our time is always governed by God's clock. Open the door to reveal the text, 'My times are in your hands' (Psalm 31:15), and explain that what makes a clock tick is the works. What makes a Christian 'tick' is that God loves him and his life, his times, are in God's hand.

Christopher Porteous
Beckenham

3 Bible Sunday

TEXT

Psalm 19.

AIM

To encourage the study of the Bible.

PREPARATION

Obtain three newspapers—the *Sun*, the *Daily Mirror* and the *Daily Mail*, preferably copies dated the week prior to the talk. Insert a double page in each paper with the following headings:

In the *Sun*:   'The heavens are telling the glory of God.'
In the *Mirror*:   1st page: 'Secret faults'
                  2nd page: 'Presumptuous sins'
In the *Mail*:   1st page: 'From God to us'
                  2nd page: 'From us to God'

PRESENTATION

I wonder what newspaper you read in your family. It's surprising how many different ones there are. How many can you think of? (List names.) In many ways the Bible, and Psalm 19 in particular, are like three of these.

1. The Sun *(show paper)*

Wherever you are in the world you can see the skies and the sun. So the sun reminds us that God has made himself known to everyone. Listen (read Psalm 19:1,4b,5,6). The writer is saying that the world of nature around us, and particularly the sun, is a constant reminder that God is alive! And that he is the Creator of the order and vastness of the heavens (show added page).

It's not enough just to look at the sun and say, 'Now I know that God is alive.' God has also given us the Bible to show us even more clearly what he is like. (Elaborate verses 7–10 if time.) So both the sun and the Bible show us that God is alive and show us what he is like.

2. The Daily Mirror *(show paper)*

I don't know how often you look into a mirror—at least once a day, I hope, and preferably before you come down to breakfast to make sure that your hair is tidy!

We see in this psalm that the Bible is just like a mirror, showing us what we are like; and it is not a beautiful picture.

(Story: tell a personal story of meeting an important visitor, and of seeing how untidy or improperly dressed you were only after you had seen the visitor, when you looked into a mirror.) Look at verse 12. Here is a picture of some of us: 'hidden faults' or 'secret faults' (show added page). We all know certain things that we think about other people, and are glad they can't hear; or certain things we do, and are glad no one can see.

Look at verse 13: 'presumptuous sins' (show added page). Things we do wrong, of which we are even proud!

Yes, the Bible not only acts like the sun, showing us what

God is like; but it also acts like a mirror, showing us what we are like.

3. *The* Daily Mail *(show paper)*

We learn from our third newspaper that God wants to be our constant friend. He speaking to us and we speaking to him; like receiving and sending letters or mail.

(i) from God to us (show added page)
Look at verses 7—11. These speak of what God is seeking to do for us: reviving us, making us wise, making us rejoice, etc. Here is God encouraging us through his word, just as we might be encouraged by a letter written to us from a friend.

(ii) from us to God (show added page)
Look at verse 14 which speaks to us of the writer's thoughts and words, asking God to make him worthy of his friendship.

Summary

Three truths which we learn from God's word:

1. Like the *Sun*, God has made himself known to us.
2. Like the *Mirror*, we can see what we are really like.
3. Like the *Mail*, God wants to be our constant friend.

You might read the *Sun*, or the *Mirror*, or the *Mail*, or even *The Times*, but the best paper to read is the Bible.

Garry Guinness
Worthing

4 Christmas Tree Lights

TEXT

Philippians 2:14–15.

AIM

To show what it means to be a Christian by means of a topical
Christmas visual aid.

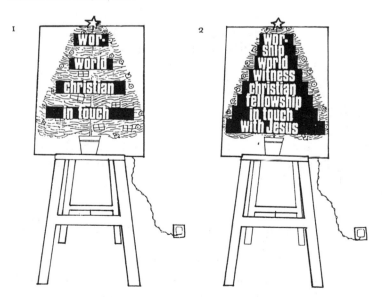

On cardboard draw the outline of a Christmas tree, which should be at least 32″ high and appear to come out of a brightly coloured pot. Put a star at the top of the tree. Divide the space of the tree into eight sections 4″ high, and write on the alternate spaces the words 'wor-', 'world', 'Christian', 'in touch', on a black background, as in diagram 1. Cover these spaces with slightly longer rectangular pieces of card, and then paint the Christmas tree, sticking on pieces of coloured fluorescent paper to represent parcels. Fold all the cards down and write on them, on a black background, the words 'ship', 'witness', 'fellowship', 'with Jesus', so that the finished tree appears as in diagram 2. The letters are more effective if cut out of fluorescent paper and stuck on. Around the tree fix a set of Christmas tree lights. Begin the talk with the cards folded up so that no words can be seen.

PRESENTATION

What is the first thing you notice about a Christmas tree? Answer: lights. The Bible compares Christians to lights. Read text and explain.

1. *Christians are in touch with Jesus*

   Christmas tree needs to be switched on or plugged in before it lights up. Christians also need to be in touch with Christ and the power of his Holy Spirit. (Turn down the bottom card.) Enlarge on the need for repentance and faith and switch on the lights.

2. *Christian fellowship*

   Once we are in touch with Christ we become part of his church. This means that we have to work together. (Turn down the next card.) We are dependent on each other. Most of you will know that if you unscrew one of these lights all the rest go out (do so to illustrate). And when one

Christian is not pulling his weight in the fellowship all the others are affected.

3. World witness

We especially notice a Christmas tree when it is lit up. The text tells us that Christians are to 'shine as lights in the world'. (Turn down the next card.) We must be seen, and seen to be different. This should show by the life we lead and by the words we say.

4. Worship

When you see a lovely Christmas tree do you say, 'What wonderful lights'? No, you say, 'What a wonderful Christmas tree,' and we must so live to glorify God that when people see us they do not say 'What wonderful people' but 'What a wonderful God we worship'. (Turn down the top card.)

Michael Botting
Editor

5 Which King?

TEXT

Luke 2:1–7.

AIM

To contrast the birth, kingship and kingdoms of two great men.

PREPARATION

Prepare drawings as illustrated, for use on Teazlegraph board.

PRESENTATION

(Lead in: at first people think you are talking about Jesus)

Contrast 1: He was born about 2000 years ago, a long way away from here. His birthday was September 23rd, 63 BC. He had a magnificent cot, with (Cot) purple blankets and silken sheets. His family lived in a smashing house, full of servants. His dad was a senator. They ran an E-type chariot. His name was Gaius Octavianus—and he had a famous uncle. Anyone know who he was? Answer: Julius Caesar. They all knew young

Gaius was going to turn out well—and when Gaius was 16 or so, his uncle Julius adopted him.

He was also born around 2000 years ago, a long way away. He was born in a cave and there was no cot for him to snuggle up in. Instead he had to make do with some straw in a cattle trough. There were no doctors or midwives. Mary, his mother, and Joseph could find nowhere better to stay than a dirty cave, used as a cattle shed. But at least it was a roof.

(Crib)

What a contrast between these two babies!

Contrast 2: He grew up to be a mighty general. After his uncle, Julius Caesar, was murdered, Gaius led an army against the murderers. He defeated Brutus. He occupied Rome. Later, he conquered Antony and Cleopatra, and by 30 BC he was

(Emperor) undisputed master of the greatest empire in the world—the Roman Empire. On January 16th, 27 BC, the Roman Senate gave him the title 'Caesar Augustus'—a title meaning 'increasing majesty'. Under him, the Roman Empire grew and grew.

He grew up to be a carpenter, working in an obscure town perched on the Judean hills. On clear days he could look down across the broad plain of Esdraelon and see the sun glinting on the armour of the Roman legions—Caesar Augustus' legions. It was Augustus who decreed the census that took Mary and Joseph to Bethlehem when Jesus was born. Jesus was about 19 when the great Emperor died. Eleven years later, when he was 30, he left the carpenter's shop and became a preacher. He never left his little country. It was just a tiny fragment of the great empire Augustus ruled. At 33 he was executed by some of another Caesar's soldiers.

(Wandering preacher)

Contrast 3: The symbol of Gaius' reign was the Roman Eagle, carried across the world by the Roman Legions. In the 41 years of his reign he ruled the roads and the seas. He stabilised the borders, enlarged the empire's territory; he brought about a political reconstruction of Rome. He promoted the arts, education and trade. By force of arms, backed by political skill and wisdom, he preserved civilisation for the next two centuries through the empire he built up. But then it faded, and began to decline.

(Roman eagle)

The symbol of Christ's reign is a Roman gibbet—the cross. It is the symbol that tells us that God cares for this world so much that he sent his only Son, the Lord of glory, to live among us and

76

(Cross) then to die for us. The Empire of Augustus, like those of Alexander, Charlemagne, Napoleon, depended on the rule of force. Jesus' kingdom is founded upon love. The empire he founded is still intact and growing after 2000 years. Of the increase of his government there shall be no end. He alone has crossed the barriers of race, time and place.

Conclusion

Which of these two babies proved to be of the greater significance, do you think? At the beginning, Gaius, one would have thought. Yet the baby in the manger finally gave significance to the Emperor, whose name is read out from Luke's Gospel every Christmastide. Towards the end of his reign, the mistaken courtiers of Augustus declared, 'A man has become god.' But Augustus was no god.

By the end of his life on earth, the followers of Jesus knew who he was. 'God has become a man.' Emmanuel, God with us. Two kings, two kingdoms. One long dead. The other still alive and his kingdom growing all the time. Across the years he still asks for what philosophers ask in vain from their students, parents in vain from their children, a leader in vain from his men: the human heart. Whose subject are you?

John Simons
Nailsea, Bristol

Editor's note

I have given this talk using a life-sized cot and crib, and with boys dressed as Emperor and Wandering Preacher who, at appropriate moments, have been handed on poles the Roman eagle and the cross.

6 Christmas Surprises

TEXT

Luke 2:8–20.

AIM

The appreciation of God's love for us, displayed in his gift of Jesus.

PREPARATION

Write on three cards: God comes at unexpected times; God does unexpected things; God uses unexpected people. Put each in a small box and wrap as Christmas present.

PRESENTATION

Point of contact

Show three small boxes, gift-wrapped as Christmas presents. 'Here are some surprises! You must have had some this Christmas!' Talk briefly about planning surprises for others, and receiving surprises ourselves. But surprises don't happen every day. We all know the thought—'Nothing exciting ever happens to *me*' or 'Monday—school, the weekly wash, off to work again!'

1. The shepherds' life

Describe their work: humdrum, monotonous (verse 8). But it was while they were at their ordinary, everyday work that God's messenger appeared to them (verse 9).

We do not have to be in some special place, or in unusual circumstances, to hear God's message. There is no special time for God to make himself known to us.

Produce from first 'surprise' parcel a folded card which opens out to show 'God comes at unexpected times'.

2. The strange message

(Verses 11,12) The Jews had long expected the Messiah. They knew how he would come—so they thought—as a Prince, or as a victorious warrior. The angel told quite a different story.

Produce from second 'surprise' parcel 'God does unexpected things'.

3. The shepherds' curiosity

They didn't send a shepherd boy to find out if it was true. They couldn't wait until morning. They would hardly have had time to find presents. They came to the stable just as they were (verses 15,16). How surprised Mary and Joseph must have been! They would not have expected visitors in the middle of the night. But—produce from third 'surprise' parcel—'God uses unexpected people'.

Conclusion

Christmas is a time of surprises. But for every surprise, someone has to be making plans—because they love us and want the best for us. The story of the first Christmas is full of surprises—all planned by God, because he loved his people so much.

Psalm 40:17, 'The Lord takes thought and plans for me' (Amplified Version); John 3:16, 'God so loved the world that he gave...' the most wonderful surprise of all!

So, we need never be depressed or afraid of that 'Monday morning feeling'; because God has given us Jesus, and because 'every perfect gift' is from him (James 1:17) we know that he is always planning something wonderful for us.

Garth Grinham
Southport

7 A Christmas Card

One of the accounts of Christ's birth. Or John 1:1–14.

To tell the story of the birth of Jesus, to show how the world has rejected him and that he has saved those who will receive him.

Make a large Christmas card out of cardboard. It has to have a cover and three pages inside, so you need altogether four pieces of white cardboard. Any picture can be used on the front, but if time is short stick on a piece of Christmas wrapping paper and write 'Christmas joy' underneath in felt pen. The first two pages inside are made with a hole so that the words written on the last page show through. Write the words 'no room' on the last page across a red heart, which can be made out of fluorescent paper so that the red also shines through the window, a background colour to the words. On the first page inside the cover write 'at the inn'; on the second page 'in the world', and on the final page 'in my heart'. A picture of the inn and of the world can also be drawn on the relevant pages.

81

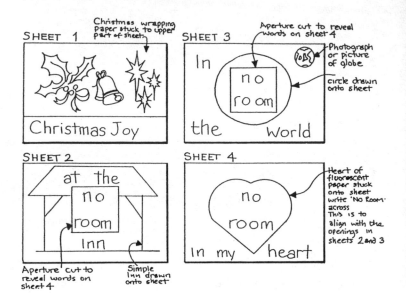

SHEET 1

Christmas wrapping paper stuck to upper part of sheet.

Christmas Joy

SHEET 3

Aperture cut to reveal words on sheet 4

Photograph or picture of globe

circle drawn onto sheet

In
no room
the World

SHEET 2

at the
no
room
Inn

Aperture cut to reveal words on sheet 4

Simple Inn drawn onto sheet

SHEET 4

Heart of fluorescent paper stuck onto sheet write 'No Room' across This is to align with the openings in sheets 2 and 3

no
room
In my heart

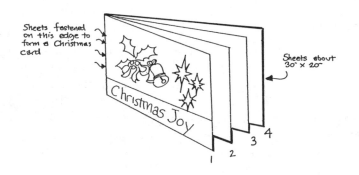

Sheets fastened on this edge to form a Christmas card

Sheets about 30" x 20"

Christmas Joy

1 2 3 4

Begin by saying that you like receiving Christmas cards. You have not been able to send one to all of them but you have brought it to church for them. Produce your card and show the front picture and 'Christmas joy'. Suggest that it was not all joy at Christmas; then turn to the first page inside and explain that there was no room for Joseph and Mary anywhere, even in the inn, and they had to go to a stable for Christ to be born. Then go on to the next page and show how often today there is no room for God in the world. Many people forget the birth of Jesus at Christmas and think only of turkey and presents. Lastly, show 'no room in my heart' and challenge them not to forget Christ but to accept him. If they do they will have Christmas joy as shown on the front of the card. A good closing hymn is 'Thou didst leave thy throne'.

Christopher Porteous
Beckenham

8 God's Christmas Gift

TEXT

2 Corinthians 9:15.

AIM

To present the message of Christmas by means of a Christmas parcel.

PREPARATION

Cover a large piece of cardboard 3'4" by 2'4" with attractive Christmas paper. Cut out some rectangular sections of the cardboard 4½" wide and about 3' long. In the gaps stick behind your parcel black cardboard or paper and, using letters cut out of fluorescent paper stuck on to the black the following words: 'What we want', 'Free to us', 'Costly to God'. In the word 'Costly' make the 'T' like a cross. Fix the rectangular pieces of cardboard back in the following way.

Obtain a good length of very thin nylon thread. This can be obtained from a shop selling angling equipment. Make some holes in your cardboard, knot the thread at one end and thread about ½" above the first gap. Bring the thread through the rectangle that has been cut out, about 1" top and bottom, and then thread it about 1" from the next rectangle. Proceed as illustrated. When the whole visual aid has been threaded the effect will be that the pieces cut out can be raised and lowered and yet still remain part of the visual aid. On a separate piece of black card put the letters of *Jesus* and have a slot above your present where *Jesus* can be fitted. Finally, put a piece of ribbon right round your gift with a coloured tag on it: 'To everyone with love from God, 2 Corinthians 9:15'.

Speak about the special feature of Christmas being the giving of presents. Refer to the Wise Men from the East with their gifts. Reveal the visual aid and refer to the label. Ask what God's special gift at Christmas time is and then refer to Jesus as God's inexpressible (or use AV's 'unspeakable') gift, quoting the text.

Many will celebrate Christmas without a thought for God's gift. The Bible says we should thank God for his great gift of the Lord Jesus. Why? Remove the ribbon from your parcel— fix the word 'Jesus' above it and in turn reveal three reasons why Jesus is the ideal gift at Christmas.

1. *What we want*

   Many people on receiving a Christmas present say, 'That is just what I wanted,' and although it is questionable whether this is always true, it is certainly true of Jesus, for we are all sinners and he came into the world to be our Saviour. 'There was no other good enough to pay the price of sin; he *only* could unlock the gate of heaven and let us in.' Unfortunately, many people do not seem to *want* Jesus; we all *need* him, but it may be only later that we realise that we want him.

2. *Free to us*

   One of the essential things about a gift is that it is free. Enlarge on the fact that we cannot earn our salvation. If God's gift were not free we would all be lost.

3. Costly to God

The reason why Jesus is free to us is because of what it cost God to give him. Point out the cross on the word 'Costly' and enlarge on the cost. Reference could be made to the

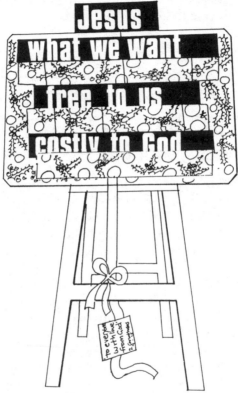

story of Abraham and his son. But God did not spare his Son. When we realise what it cost God to give us his great Christmas gift we should want to receive the Lord Jesus Christ (John 1:12–13) and to say 'Thanks be to God for his inexpressible gift.'

Michael Botting
Editor

9 Christmas Crackers (for Christmas Day)

TEXT

John 1:1–14 or Luke 2:8–16.

AIM

To teach the real meaning of Christmas.

PREPARATION

Make six Christmas crackers (kits for this purpose may be purchased from: D.I.Y. Crackers, 85 Princes Street, Southend on Sea, Essex SS1 1PT, 0702 338053).

The crackers should contain:
1. The traditional items; ie, a paper hat, a toy, a trinket, a lucky charm, and a motto or joke.
2. A baby doll.
3. A ring.
4. A cross—of the kind worn on a chain.
5. A crown made of paper thin enough to fit inside the barrel of the cracker.
6. A piece of paper with a Bible verse on it—John 1:14—'The Word became flesh and made his dwelling among us,' or Luke 2:10–11: 'I bring you good news of great joy... today...a Saviour has been born to you; he is Christ the Lord.'

Make cards for display on Teazlegraph board of the following words: toy; trinket; charm; hat; motto; joke; baby; ring; cross; crown; Good News. Alternatively, these words could be written on an OHP.

PRESENTATION

Ask children to suggest things that make Christmas dinner special. When crackers are mentioned produce the first one and explain that you've had a go at making one yourself, and ask for a volunteer to pull it with you. Before pulling the cracker ask what we would expect to find inside a good cracker, and display cards—toy, hat, etc—as appropriate. Then pull cracker and reveal paper hat, toy, trinket, charm, and motto/joke. (Add any cards to display if not already mentioned.)

Next, call for a second volunteer; pull a cracker and reveal a baby doll. (Put card with 'baby' on it next to 'toy' on board.) Talk about Christmas being Jesus' birthday, why we give presents, and explain that Jesus is not just for Christmas but for life. Refer also to Jesus being God come down to earth.

Third volunteer pulls the third cracker to reveal the ring: a symbol of love. Place card with 'ring' on it next to 'trinket' on board. Talk about how much God loves us, and that by following Jesus we can know that love and share it with others.

Fourth volunteer pulls the fourth cracker to reveal the cross. Place card with 'cross' on it next to 'charm' on board. Talk about how many people rely on luck, horoscopes, etc, and then explain how Jesus became a man and died for everybody on the cross so that all might be forgiven and enter into a special loving relationship with God, which is infinitely better than relying on chance, or fate.

Fifth cracker reveals the hat: show that it is in the form of a crown. Place 'crown' next to 'hat' on board. Explain how Jesus rose from the dead and now reigns for ever as King, and how we must give him our whole-hearted allegiance.

Last cracker reveals 'motto'. Place 'Good News' next to 'motto' on board. Talk about how the message of Christmas is the best news ever for this world. Refer to Jesus as Emmanuel—God is with us—and how he can transform our lives if we will let him. Perhaps, to conclude, get all the congregation to repeat the text to their neighbour.

N.B. It may be found preferable to rearrange the order of opening the crackers after the first one.

David McIntosh
Ellesmere Port

10 The Birth of Jesus Christ

TEXT

Any passage from the gospels on the birth of Jesus.

AIM

To tell the story of Christ's birth and explain the reason for his coming to man.

This visual aid is made out of four pieces of cardboard on to which are put headlines for children to show to the congregation. The headlines can be made from advertisements for the local paper displayed outside newsagents, by cutting newsprint from advertisements or by writing with felt pen. The headlines read: 'Baby born in stable report'; 'The prince of peace'; 'Family saved from disaster'; and 'Good news'. The first three could be headed 'Bethlehem Journal' and the fourth 'News for the World'.

PRESENTATION

Ask four children before the talk each to bring up a headline when you ask them. Then tell the story of Christ's birth by bringing in each headline as you proceed. Begin by asking the name of your local newspaper and then suggest that the local paper for the town where Jesus was born would be 'The Bethlehem Journal'.

Baby born in stable

Tell how Mary and Joseph came to Bethlehem and point out that if a baby were born in a stable today it might still get in the paper, because babies are not usually born in such dirty places.

The Prince of Peace

Explain that it was even more extraordinary that the person to be born there was not just any baby but a very special one: God's own Son, called the Prince, a King, the Prince of Peace. He came to bring God's peace to men's hearts, to give peace to those who were troubled about their relationship to God, to bring peace on earth where men will love and serve him.

Family saved from disaster

Tell how Joseph and Mary had to flee from Herod, who would not have another prince in his realm, because he did not want the Prince of Peace, as many do not want him today. However, God saved the Holy Child.

Good News

It was Good News, not just because a baby was born, or because God saved him from Herod, but Good News because God sent his Son into the world to save us, to find us and to bring us to God.

Christopher Porteous
Beckenham

11 'Ring out the Old Year, Ring in the New'

TEXTS

Exodus 28: 33–34; Joshua 24:14–15.

AIM

To say goodbye and turn from a past year and welcome and turn to a new year. Committing ourselves to God for the coming year.

This talk could take place in a Covenant service as used in the Free Church tradition.

PREPARATION

1. If you have church bells arrange for them to ring on (a) New Year's Eve, (b) before the service, and (c) have a ringer on hand to toll a bell for you as required.
2. This is an object talk. You need a variety of bells. The more the merrier. Here are some suggestions: Swiss cow bell, school teacher's bell, dinner table bell, alarm clock bell (not buzzer!).

PRESENTATION

1. There are all sorts of bells—here are some of them. What do you think they are and what is the purpose of each of

these bells? Then hold the bells up one at a time and let congregation supply the answers.

2. If you have church bells it might be helpful to give a brief history of your bells and their inscriptions. Maybe even interview your bell tower captain.

3. The first mention of bells in the Bible is in Exodus 28:33–34—the golden bells on the High Priest's robes. The older members of the congregation might recall that there was a Christian hymnbook called *Golden Bells* whose title came from this verse.

4. The High Priest's bells on his robes were a significant sound. They were a constant reminder to him of the importance of his worship of God and his walk with God. Because Jesus is our Great High Priest (Hebrews) this applies to us today as we worship the Lord and walk with him in our daily lives.

5. So as we ring out an old year and ring in a new year let us remember how the bells help us. Their purpose is to act as a stimulating sound for everyone who hears them.

   (a) To remind—consideration of the past.

   (b) To rejoice—celebration in the present.

   (c) To resolve—commitment for the future.

6. Joshua renewed his commitment to God for himself and his family at Shechem. There are times when this is right and proper for God's people. A New Year is one of those occasions. We can look back from the present and then look forward into the New Year. The month of January, named after the Roman God Janus, who faced two directions, is a good month to recommit ourselves, just as Joshua did with his family for the future.

Ray Adams
Redditch

12   The Meaning of Epiphany

TEXT

Titus 2: 11–14.

AIM

To teach about the two epiphanies or appearings of Jesus
Christ and how we should live between them.

PREPARATION

Cut out of cardboard a large circular disc, say 12″ radius, and
paint it black. Paste onto the disc, as illustrated, a large circle
of yellow fluorescent paper to represent the sun. Next paste
pictures of a manger, a cross and an open tomb to represent
the first coming of Jesus. There should then be a gap followed
by a gold figure among clouds to represent the second coming
of Jesus.

In the centre of the gap have a piece of black Velcro
backing and cut out a separate large question mark with
Velcro on the back so that it can be stuck onto the disc.

Cut out a rectangular piece of card at least 2″ wider than
the diameter of the disc and at least 1″ deeper than its radius
and having at the centre of the top a small semi-circle of card
as illustrated. This second card should also be painted black.

The two cards should now be joined together with a very

strong drawing pin that goes through the rectangle in the bottom centre of the small semi-circle and through the centre of the large disc and hence onto, say, a Teazlegraph board. In the space on the back of the rectangle where the circular disc does not come should be stuck some card of the same thickness

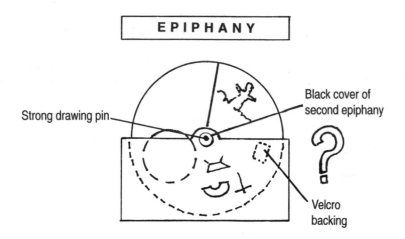

as the disc and Velcro stuck to it. Some thin black card should also be clipped to cover over the Second Coming scene.

When you begin the talk the disc should be in such a position that the sun is just on the verge of appearing. Have the word EPIPHANY on card with Velcro on the back.

If at all possible have the whole text above on an OHP acetate, but split into four sections, namely:

'For the grace...all men.'

'It teaches...present age,'

'while we wait...Saviour, Jesus'

'Christ, who...what is good.'

Ask what the brightest light is that we can see. Mention that often we cannot see it, but that does not mean it is not there. Make reference to dawn when the sun makes its appearance or **EPIPHANY** (from the Greek word). Put the word at the top of the Teazlegraph board. Move the disc so that the sun comes into view.

1. The first Epiphany

Assuming that this talk is being given around Epiphany time make reference to it and ask what event we especially associate with it. (The visit of the Wise Men.) Before Jesus came the world was dark through ignorance and superstition, sin and death, and with little hope of resurrection. Jesus came to bring light to Jews and Gentiles. Throw onto the OHP the beginning and end of the text. Move the disc so that the first epiphany pictures appear and say that when Jesus came he was rather like the sun making an appearance or epiphany. He had been in existence from all eternity, being part of the Godhead, but was now coming into view. Quote the parts of the text on the screen and comment appropriately about the manger, cross, empty tomb and ascension.

2. The second Epiphany

Place the third part of the text on the OHP ('While we wait...) and move the disc so that the Second Coming scene becomes visible (having removed the small piece of black paper that covered it). Briefly comment that whenever we recite the Creed we state that we believe Jesus will one day return to this earth, as he promised, not in humility, as at the first Epiphany, but in great triumph. Quote that part of the text.

3. *Now*

Place the large question mark on the disc and the remaining piece of text on the OHP. Comment on the sort of life Christians should be living between the Epiphanies, especially letting their light shine (see Matthew 5:16) that others may hear about the first Epiphany and be ready for the second.

A very effective way to end is to use the brilliant light bulb illustration in Talk 57.

Michael Botting
Editor

13 Home and Family
(suitable for Mothering Sunday)

Texts

Deuteronomy 6:4–9; 1 Timothy 1:5; 3:14,15; 2 Timothy 3:10–17.

Aim

To show the importance God places upon home and family.

Preparation

Prepare large models or cards as shown, of a house, a family, a heart and a Bible.

Presentation

Point of contact

Talk about 'no place like home'. Produce large house-shaped model or card. But emphasise that the home is incomplete without people to live in it.

1. God means us to live together (Deuteronomy 6:7)

Produce figures of family and place them superimposed on house. Emphasise:

(i) how God speaks of the family unit, and of such homely things as parents and children talking, sitting, walking, going to bed and getting up;

(ii) how we should value as God's gifts things that go to make up a happy home, and not neglect them, e.g. being together indoors, out of doors.

2. *God means us to love together* (Deuteronomy 6:4)

Produce heart shape and place it superimposed on family. Emphasise:

(i) a command

(ii) to be taken seriously (Matthew 22:38; Mark 12:31)

(iii) with heart, soul and might

    (iv) when we love him, we love one another (Mark 12:30–31; 1 John 4:21).

Stress how we love him together by
(i)   praying to him as a family
(ii)   witnessing for him as a family
(iii) using our home in his service
(iv) worshipping together as a family in church.

3. *God means us to learn together* (Deuteronomy 6:6–8)

Produce Bible card and place it superimposed on heart shape.
Emphasise essential need for family Bible reading.
(i)   Bible to be known by parents (verse 6)
(ii)   Bible to be taught to children (verse 7)
(iii) Bible to be stored in minds (e.g. 'learned by heart', verse 6)
(iv) Bible to be shared with others (verse 9).

Conclusion

Encourage daily Bible reading system (e.g. Scripture Union. Have supply of notes available.)

Sing as congregation the hymn: 'Happy the home that welcomes you, Lord Jesus.'

Garth Grinham
Southport

14   Happy Families
(Suitable for Infant Baptism service, or
Mothering Sunday, or both)

TEXT

John 1:10–13 (RSV).

AIM

To distinguish between the different families to which we all
can belong.

PREPARATION

Prepare a large board, covered with white paper, into which
pins can be stuck. Three silhouette models are needed, large
enough for all to see: a home, a church (your church building,
if possible), and a cross, to depict the three families (they will
be placed at the top of columns 1, 2 and 3 respectively). Then
cut out silhouette models of men, women and children and a
pram in bright contrasting paper (e.g. green, brown, grey and
black) large enough to be seen. A simple silhouette of a man
can be drawn; fold from top to bottom, and cut several pieces
of paper at a time. When opened out it will form a regularly
shaped figure, which can be varied slightly to resemble a
woman and reduced slightly to resemble a child. You will need
three labels, reading 'born', 'baptism' and 'born again'. Each
silhouette or card is punched with holes so that it can be

hooked on the pins suitably positioned in the board. Teazlegraph can equally well be used, if available.

PRESENTATION

Three different families:
>   Our home family (place house in position)
>   Our church family (place church in position)
>   God's family (place cross in position)

1. *Our home family* (to which we all belong)

Place father, mother, son, daughter and baby (pram) silhouettes in position. They should all be of one colour paper,
e.g. bright green. Ask for a name, and settle for 'Mr and
Mrs Green'. We are all born into this family. Mothering
Sunday fits in here, as we say thank you to our mothers and
give them a special kiss. Gifts of flowers given on Mothering
Sunday are a way of saying 'thank you'.

2. *Our church family*

Meet Mr and Mrs Brown, their son and daughter (use
brown paper). They all four go to church together when
there is a Family Service; otherwise the son is in Pathfinders
and the daughter is in Explorers (use local equivalents).
Mrs Green goes to church too (take the silhouette and hang
it beside Mrs Brown, leaving a gap for Mr Green in
between). Master Green also goes to Pathfinders, and Miss
Green goes to Explorers (place them alongside the Brown
children).

Mrs Green's baby is also brought to church each week,
because they welcome babies and have a creche for them, or
else they come into Family Services too (move green pram
to column 2). But the family is sad because Mr Green
doesn't go to church, not even when there is a Family
Service (leave his silhouette hanging by itself at home).

Then Mr and Mrs Brown had a baby, and wanted their

baby to be received as part of the church family; and so the baby is baptised. All the rest of the church family are at the Family Service, and say together, 'We receive this child into the congregation of Christ's flock' (place the Brown pram in position).

3. *God's family*

This family is not always the same as the one we have just considered. Mrs Brown had loving Christian parents who helped her to know Jesus. She is a real Christian (move her silhouette across to the third family). You see, her parents were Christians before her: how much we owe to our parents and grandparents—their love and their prayers! The parents have died and gone to be with Jesus, but are still part of the family (place Mr and Mrs Grey on either side of the cross). Mrs Brown prayed for her family and one by one she had the joy of seeing them come to know Christ. First the son, then the daughter believed (move them to the third family). The baby is covered by the mother's faith, though still a baby (move the pram). But sadly Mr Brown does not believe (leave him behind in column 2). Mrs Brown is still praying for him.

Mrs Brown then told Mrs Green about Jesus—a cross because Christ died; an empty cross because Christ rose and is alive. Mrs Green became a Christian (move her to column 3, next to Mrs Brown). Mrs Green prayed for her children, and both became believers (move them to next column); the baby in the pram is again covered by the mother's faith because it is a baby (move pram to column 3).

Mrs Green is now praying for her husband, that he will come to church and find Christ. Notice that in this family, God's family, the relationships cross the generations: i.e. those who are *with Christ* (like Mr and Mrs Grey), and those who are *in Christ* (like Mrs Green and Mrs Brown and their children). See 'from generation to generation' (Psalm 100:4,

Prayer Book). More than that, the family extends outwards as well as up and down, for there are those of every nation, every race and colour who belong to God's family (hang a black silhouette of a man beside Mrs Green). What a *wonderful* family this is to which we belong by faith in Christ! It is 'eternal' (from generation to generation) and 'universal' (of every nation and colour).

Conclusion: How do we become members of these families?

1. Our home family — we are *born* into it
2. Our church family — we enter it by *baptism*
3. God's family — we are *born again* into it, or as the Bible puts it, by 'believing' and 'receiving'

(Hang at the foot of each column the cards appropriately named as they are mentioned.)

To belong to one family does not necessarily mean that we belong automatically to another.

Stephen Trapnell
Marlborough

15   Palm Sunday

Text

Matthew 21:1–17.

Aim

To challenge people to make—and keep—Jesus as King of their lives.

Preparation

Traditional Teazlegraph figures for the following people or groups: Jesus on a donkey, children, disciples, soldiers, Pharisees, Pilate, crowds and a cross. Cut two large pieces of card (20″ x 30″ tall) each cut identically to make the outline of a heart (cardioid) shape. For part one of the talk, they can be placed as to make an oval representing the city walls of Jerusalem. For part two, these can be rearranged, with one reversed, to make the shape of a human heart. Put Teazlegraph stickers on both sides of these two pieces of cardboard, as one side will need to be reversed in order to change the oval to the heart.

PRESENTATION

1. Jesus came to Jerusalem. (Place the two pieces of card outline to make an oval for the city walls and Jesus on a donkey.) He was welcomed in to the city. Here he meets different groups of people.

   Draw out the answers by questions, and as appropriate put the figures on the board background within the city walls.

   The children welcomed him. He taught in the temple. He healed in the temple. His disciples followed him. The crowds listened to him. The Pharisees plotted against him. The soldiers arrested him. Pilate condemned him. They then sent him outside the city walls to be crucified. (Put cross on the outside.)

   How sad that he was welcomed in with such joy—and sent outside to be crucified.

2. Let's change the walls now to represent the human heart. When Jesus comes near you—do you invite him in? What sort of reception does he get? Are you perhaps like the Pharisees, very religious and righteous in your good deeds? Are you like the crowds, who love Jesus when it is popular, but perhaps later cry 'Crucify him'? Are you like the soldiers who think they are so strong and right, but reject Jesus? Are you like the children, enthusiastic and happy at the beginning but unable to change things? Are you like the disciples who stick with Jesus, even through failure?

   I hope you have welcomed Jesus in as King—and you keep him there as King. It would be so sad if you wanted him to leave, or you tried to crucify him again to get rid of him.

   Make appeal or challenge as appropriate.

David Williams
Cheltenham

16   Good Friday (1)

TEXT

John 9:5.

AIM

To show that Jesus is the light of the world, and that he can never be put out.

METHOD

With the aid of candles, dramatise how the darkness nearly overcame the light of the world.

PREPARATION

Prepare a large tray with a giant red candle in the centre, and twelve white ones on the circumference. Fix them so that they are steady and yet can be removed at will. Have one further white candle which you give to a member of the congregation before the service. You will also need a box of matches, and one black cardboard cylinder, just taller than the red candle, and large enough to go over it.

Introduction

'I am the light of the world.' Jesus said these words to his followers after they had met a man who had been blind all his life. When he had said this, he spat on the ground and made clay (rather like a medicine), and rubbed it on to the man's eyes. The man went and washed and came back seeing! A wonderful event that actually happened! But when Jesus said, 'I am the light of the world,' he wasn't just or even primarily talking of physical sight. He was speaking of those who are in spiritual darkness—those who can't see the right thing to do, those who don't know how to be forgiven by God, when they know they have done wrong. There are many people who say, 'I can't see the purpose of life. I don't know where I'm going.' To them Jesus says, 'I am the light of the world.'

Development

It all started even before the first Christmas, but then Jesus was born into the world—the light of the world began to shine in the world. (Light red candle on tray.)

One by one Jesus called together his followers to act as lights too. 'You are the light of the world,' he said to them (Matthew 5:14).

Light the twelve candles by bringing them up to the red candle. As you light them, say something about each one: Simon called Peter, and his brother Andrew; James and John the sons of Zebedee; Philip and Bartholomew; Matthew and Thomas; James the son of Alphaeus; Thaddaeus; Simon the Zealot; Judas Iscariot who betrayed Jesus.

For three years they were together, seeking to understand just how they could reflect the light of Jesus and themselves be lights in the world. And then came the last week leading up to Good Friday. Judas was the first to go out (blow his candle out), and one by one they all forsook Jesus and fled (blow all the white candles out—filling in details if you wish as you put them out).

Last of all Jesus, alone on the cross, died; the light of the world was no longer seen in the world. (Cover the red candle with black cylinder, but be careful not to put the light out. Be sure to practise this beforehand! The congregation will think that the light has gone out, but it will go on burning if you are careful.)

Matthew records that there was darkness over the whole land at this time (Matthew 27:45), and with the light of the world out, it was dark indeed. Jesus was dead and they buried his body.

Easter Day

But then on the first day of the week, while it was still early in the morning, Mary Magdalene went to the tomb where they had laid the body of Jesus. It was gone! And then, there he was in front of her, Jesus the light of the world! Others too saw him alive. He is alive, no one and nothing can put out the light of the world. (Take the cylinder off the candle, which should still be burning.)

Perhaps you are saying, 'I long to be a light, a candle for Jesus Christ in the world. What must I do?' You must come to him and allow him to give his light to you. (Ask member of congregation to come forward with candle, but don't light it yet.) Before I light the candle, I must tell you a story.

Story

Some years ago in the city of Florence in Italy, lived a wealthy man who not only owned his own castle, but even his own little chapel in the castle. He wanted the chapel to be the very best, and employed the famous artist Gonzoli to paint the walls and ceiling. There were no windows in the chapel, which was lit by artificial lighting. Candles lit up the beautiful little place, but this light was really not good enough. The time came when the owner realised that the only answer was to make a window in one of the walls, even though it would mean destroying one of the paintings. The best place to have the window was at the East end, above the beautifully carved table. The picture above the table was a portrait of himself that Gonzoli had painted! The workmen took their hammers and chisels, and the painting was soon in pieces: the hole grew bigger and bigger until the space was wide enough for a window, and the light streamed into the chapel!

Our lives are like that, for if the Lord Jesus, the light of the world, is to shine into our lives, then the picture of 'us' must go. He will come in, if we let him take the very best place in our lives. Are you prepared for this? Then you must say a prayer like this: 'Lord Jesus, I am prepared for you to have the best place in my life; thank you for overcoming the darkness of our sins on the cross, thank you for coming alive again on the first Easter day, thank you that you are alive now. Come into my life today.'

Light the candle held by the member of the congregation.

Garry Guinness
Worthing

17   Good Friday (2)

TEXT

Luke 23:39–49.

AIM

To tell the story of Good Friday and explain why Christ had to die.

PREPARATION

The visual aid is made out of three sheets of cardboard using the idea of the different editions of a newspaper: 'Early Edition', 'Late Edition' and 'Late Extra'. Also obtain an advertisement for 'Moneymail' from any shop which sells the *Daily Mail*. The wording on the three sheets of cardboard is as follows:

'Early Edition. Moneymail. Saviour Sold.'
'Late Edition. Robber Released.'
'Late Extra. Thief Forgiven.'

PRESENTATION

Give your advertisements to three children who are to bring them up in turn as you tell the story of Good Friday. We are going to write possible headlines for the paper for Good Friday. The first headline, of course, deals with the selling of Jesus for thirty pieces of silver by Judas. The second deals with the release of Barabbas instead of Jesus, and the third with the two thieves on the crosses next to Jesus. During the talk you draw the comparison that the price of selling Jesus was thirty pieces of silver, but the price of his saving us for eternity was his death on the cross. Point out that an undeserving robber was released and one who had done no wrong died in his place. So with us, Christ died in our place when we deserved death. Show how the thief who was forgiven said the same thing, namely that he deserved death but Christ did not, and show that it is never too late in this life to have faith in Christ. To end the talk, have three pieces of black cardboard with fluorescent lettering on them reading 'He died' 'to save' 'us all', and stick these over the three headings.

Christopher Porteous
Beckenham

18 Pay Day

Romans 6:23.

Aim

To explain the meaning of the cross, by means of a visual aid, which would be especially topical if used on Good Friday.

Preparation

Either simply have a five pound note available or, if you or a member of your congregation has the necessary ability, paint a large note on a piece of cardboard with a piece of card that can be pulled out from one side, with the words 'Wages for Work' on it. On the back of the five pound note have a skull and crossbones and the words 'I promise to pay death', and pull out 'Wages of Sin'.

Presentation

Begin by talking about pay-day. Show five pound note and 'Wages for Work'. Talk about the five pound note as being a promise from the chief cashier of the Bank of England to pay five pounds sterling, and comment on the Sovereign's head appearing on the note as a guarantee of its trustworthiness.

But work is not the only thing for which we deserve a wage. Turn over the visual aid if you are using the larger one and show that God promises that the wages for sin is death.

Illustrate this from the story of Adam and Eve, Achan, King Saul, Judas, etc. But we don't have to look just to the Bible for illustrations. We know it in practical experience—the misuse of money, sex and drugs teaches us this. Go on to say, however, that this Friday is *pay day* in another sense. On Good Friday Jesus, the sinless Son of God, deliberately allowed sinful men to nail him to a cross, and while he hung from it God his Father turned his face from him and allowed him to suffer hell—that is spiritual death—for us. Jesus died the death you and I deserve. He paid the wages of sin once and for all.

There was no other good enough
To pay the price of sin:
He only could unlock the gate
Of heaven and let us in.

Now all those who repent of their sins and believe on Jesus
Christ as their Saviour are promised the free gift of eternal life
from God—and God never breaks a promise.

Does Friday mean pay day for you?

Michael Botting
Editor

19   The Redemption Shop

TEXT

Ephesians 1:7.

AIM

To illustrate the significance of the death of Christ.

PREPARATION

Paint a much enlarged green shield stamp on card. Stick another piece of card of similar size on the back, but ensure that none of the glue comes 5″ from the top or 5″ down the middle. With a sharp blade cut the green shield painting from top to bottom 2½″ either side of the centre so that only the shield is cut, but not the backing card. Similarly cut 5″ from the top of the shield. Cut the central piece of card horizontally about a quarter from the top. Fix the four pieces of the shield to make a large cross using some strong paper or sellotape as a hinge. Paper the entire cross with red fluorescent paper and write on the text as illustrated. When beginning the talk have the extremities of the cross folded over so that the green shield appears complete and the cross is not obvious. Or a much simpler visual aid can be used by showing a book of trading stamps from your local garage or Cooperative Society, and drawing a cross on the blackboard or overhead projector with the text as shown. Also have some coal, salt, water and chalk available.

PRESENTATION

Explain how Jesus was always talking about very ordinary things with which his hearers were very familiar. If he were the preacher here today he might well have used the illustration of trading stamps with which most of us are familiar. Let me explain briefly how the system works. The stamps belong to the trading company and are bought by your local shops or garages and given away to you when you buy from them. If the trading company are to get back their stamps they have to redeem them or buy them back from you. They will give you money, but most people prefer a gift. This takes place at the redemption shop. (Show large stamp with cross not visible.)

This idea of redeeming is nothing new. For example, slavery was a very common thing in the world at one time. However, slaves could sometimes be freed if a redemption price was paid. The famous Pastor Richard Wurmbrand, who spent some thirteen years in a communist prison camp, was redeemed by some Norwegian Christians for the price of £2,500.

How much are we worth? In one sense not very much. We are made up of coal, salt, chalk and water equal to about £1! But in another sense we are worth much more. Once we belonged to God. He created us, but through sin we have become enemies of God (Romans 5:10—this may need some further explanation, especially as Jesus is often said, quite rightly, to be our friend).

We are astray from God like trading stamps are astray from the trading company. But God loves us very much. He wants to have us back in his company. However, to do so he had to offer a redemption price—none other than the blood of Christ, his only begotten Son. Explain more about Good Friday and Christ's death on the cross. As the famous Good Friday hymn puts it:

There was no other good enough
To pay the price of sin;
He only could unlock the gate
Of heaven, and let us in.

God bought us back by the death of his Son. Or, as the Apostle Paul puts it, 'We have redemption through his blood.' (Unfold cross on visual aid.) What an amazing price God has put on you and me. Surely we should want to belong to him again who loves us so much. If we turn to him and put our trust in all he has done for us on the cross, God receives us back. We belong to him again—we are redeemed. Redemption, then, is the way in which a person gets back what originally belonged to him. At a very great cost God has paid the price to redeem you. Are you willing to come back to him?

If time permits, the classic story could be told of the boy who lost the model boat he had made and then saw it for sale in a toy shop. To get his boat back he had to buy it (i.e. redeem it). The boat was therefore his by creation and redemption, as we are in our relationship to God.

Michael Botting
Editor

20   The Meaning of the Cross

TEXT

Luke 22:39–46.

AIM

To show that the cross is the only escape route from the power
and penalty of sin.

PREPARATION

Prepare pictures for Teazlegraph board, as shown. Small plastic canoe and aeroplane can be used, with Velcro disc on the
base.

PRESENTATION

Scene 1

Show a large picture of the two children, paddling along in their canoe in a quiet section of the river. Suddenly a light aircraft appears overhead, banking and waggling its wings. Children realise this must be their father and older brother, who had hired a light plane for the day. Children wave back, but give no heed to plane's efforts to warn them of danger (weir) round next corner of river. This is clearly visible to those in the plane up above, but the children at river level are quite unaware of danger.

Finally the plane swoops low ahead of canoe, and older brother jumps into river from thirty feet. Brother is killed, hitting a rock. But the children are now alerted by their brother's sacrifice of himself. They feel the rapids sweeping the canoe, and hear the thunder of the weir ahead. Then they spot a narrow exit stream the far side of the river.

Scene 2

Show the overall scene on Teazlegraph board. Father in plane is still anxiously circling, watching to see whether children will respond and escape. Mark the spot where the older brother died with a cross, and show the children battling to heed the warning, by turning from the broad sweep of the racing river that leads to the weir (destruction), to the narrow exit on the far bank that leads to safety (and life). Move canoe gradually across river while relating. Will the warning be heeded? Will they make it?

Scene 3

On separate board, if available, show how Easter is like this story. God the Father loves us, and so does his Son, Jesus. Jesus is like an older brother to us. The Father and the Son see, from above, that we are on a dangerous course, headed towards disaster. Mankind has been given many warnings, but men have not heeded them. So God came right down among us, to alert us and show us the way out. Jesus came and lived among us, and at Easter gave his life as a sacrifice for us.

(Show picture of Jesus on the cross.) When you see Jesus on the cross, he is laying down his life for very special reasons—as did the brother who leaped from the aeroplane (but with Jesus it was no accident when he died). We must try to understand them. Here are three of the meanings of the cross:

1. A warning to all. Explain the pull of sin, likening it to the quickening pace of the river; explain the serious results of continuing on the way of sin; say that *all* travel this way, and all need the warning, without exception. We all have to pass the cross in life, where the Son laid down his life. But will we heed it?

2. A cure for all. How does the death of Jesus make us better? How does it heal us from sin? You remember how Jesus, before his death, prayed, 'Father, if it be possible, take this cup from me. Nevertheless, not my will but thine be done.' What did he mean by the *cup*? Why did he shrink from it? Explain: not real cup, but way of saying how much it cost him to bear our sin.

   Illustrate by showing one large bottle pouring its hateful contents into cup. This bottle filled by many small bottles, which are our sins. Yours and mine. The poison of our sin is taken from us to him. So much the Son of God loves us. The cross *is* a cure for all—all those who ask to be healed.

3. An invitation to all. The cross warns us. The cross cures us, as we put our trust in Jesus. But it also points us to the narrow way, the different route in life. Jesus invites us to travel that way—with him. It has a different destination—eternal life.

Conclusion

Those who heed the warning, experience the cure and accept the invitation discover the most thrilling way through life.

Who today will heed the message of the cross, and turn to the life to which Jesus calls us?

John Simons
Nailsea, Bristol

21   Jesus Died for Me

TEXTS

Romans 3:22, GNB; Romans 3:25, GNB.

AIM

To enjoy the wonderful gift of forgiveness earned for us by Jesus.

PREPARATION

You will need:
- eight hand-sized pieces of coloured card cut in irregular shapes—they are to represent stains on clothing, e.g, grass, chocolate, blood, mud, milk, tea, coke, coffee
- eight hand-sized pieces of white card cut in irregular shapes. Print boldly one word on each card: steal (or pinch), lie (or fib), hit, greedy, lazy, cheat, temper, cheek
- eight pieces of Blutak
- a large piece of card 24″ x 18″ (or OHP acetate) with a washing machine drawn on one side, and the word 'Mummy' on the other
- a large piece of card 24″ x 18″ (or OHP acetate) with a cross drawn on it and the word 'Jesus' on the other.

1. Tell a funny story which describes how you once got truly filthy. Mine involves cycling into a canal when a teenager; slowly sinking into the mud while upright; smelly bubbles and weed; reaching the towpath without falling over; being wet from my armpits, and muddy from my waist; cycling home with mud flying everywhere; finding my family in the garden whose laughter at my state was such that they didn't speak to me for ten minutes—and when they did it was to say I wasn't going into the house to the bathroom like that. I needed to undress and be hosed down first.

2. Ask for occasions when members of the congregation have been very dirty. Hope the churchwarden or an elder can oblige. Remember *all* have sinned and fallen short of the glory of God. Depending on time allow two or three *brief* tales.

    Ask what the worst stains are you can get, then proceed as follows:
    - Grass—get child to hold green card stain to knee.
    - Chocolate—another child holds brown card stain to tummy.
    - Blood—child holds red card to shoulder blade.

    In due course you have eight people/children in funny postures holding stains onto their clothes.

3. Observe that all eight people have the same problem. Ask for the solution. Hold up the large card with a washing machine on it. Silently turn it round to reveal the word 'Mummy'. Note she does all the work for us. (This is, I know, sexist. However, note that moral indignation is also applied at point 5 below.) Tell the eight to relax, and ask one to hold the picture of the washing machine.

4. Explain that there are other stains. Ask who has been cheeky so far that day, or lazy or greedy. Ask them to hold the appropriate white card to themselves. In due course

you have eight people/children holding eight sins against themselves.

5. These people have a problem too. What is their solution? Hold up the large card with a cross on it. Invite the eight to blutak their sins to the cross, or write them on the OHP. Observe that someone else is taking the blame for them. Turn the card to reveal who. Read verses from Romans 3.

6. Prayer: Thank you for mums to make us clean and ready for our friends.
Thank you for Jesus to make us clean and ready for God.

Matthew Grayshon
Hanwell, London

22   Easter (1) The Broken Easter Egg

TEXT

Acts 1:3.

AIM

To convey as simply as possible the evidence for the Resurrection illustrated by using a broken Easter egg.

PREPARATION

Construct out of cardboard a large flat Easter egg, say about 3′ 4″ maximum length and 2′ 3″ maximum width. Divide the egg up into five pieces as illustrated, the centre piece having the words, preferably in yellow fluorescent paper, 'Jesus Risen' on it. The other four pieces, which could be covered with different coloured fluorescent paper, should have the words, and possibly illustrations, of the 'Empty Tomb', 'Bible', 'The Church', and 'Changed Disciples'. Three other pieces of white card similar in shape to the piece in the centre of the egg, but not identical, should have the words on them 'Fable', 'Fancy' and 'Body Stolen'. Either fix the pieces on to a Teazlegraph board or fix some drawing pins in discreet places to hold each piece in place. The visuals could also be done on an OHP.

Explain that there are various reasons for believing the Easter story. Why should we doubt the biblical account, remembering that the writers got no royalties for their work and in some cases suffered and died for their testimony to Jesus? No one

who has studied the evidence with an open mind can deny that the tomb was empty. Comment on the condition of the grave-clothes, the remarkable change in the frightened disciples, and the coming into existence of the Christian church. As you talk about each of these things, place the different parts of the egg on to a blackboard so that the egg is gradually formed in front of the congregation's eyes, but with the centre piece missing.

How do we account for these facts? One suggestion was that the disciples stole the body. Refer to Matthew 28:11–15, and say how impossible the idea really is. Attempt to fit the piece 'Body Stolen' into the egg and ask whether it fits. Next discuss the idea of 'Fancy', explaining how the disciples may have imagined that they saw Jesus. Point out that in fact they were not expecting to see him and on a number of occasions mistook him for someone else first (e.g. Mary Magdalene in the garden, two disciples on the Emmaus Road), which is not the way hallucinations work. Attempt to fit 'Fancy' into the egg, but unsuccessfully. Next try 'Fable', explaining how someone has suggested that the Christian story evolved rather mysteriously like many fables associated with other religions. Point out that there is plenty of evidence in Israel today for the existence of Jesus as well as plenty of historical evidence. 'This was not done in a corner,' the Apostle Paul told King Agrippa. Attempt to fit in 'Fable', also unsuccessfully.

Finally, pick up the shape 'Jesus risen' and discover that it fits. Briefly recap how this is the one explanation of the various items round the egg and ask whether the congregation know the risen Jesus for themselves.

Michael Botting
Editor

23 Easter (2) God's Easter Egg

Based on 1 Corinthians 15:1–4, 55–56.

Aim and Method

To show the meaning of Easter by means of a large Easter egg and various objects that can be pulled out of it.

Preparation

Draw on cardboard a large egg (about 3′ 4″ maximum height and 2′ 3″ maximum width). Paint the egg with attractive colours and put ribbon round the middle. Cut three rectangular strips of cardboard out of the egg and write the following

words on paper to stick behind the gaps: 'Death defeated', 'Sinners saved', 'Life loosed'. Replace the rectangular pieces of card that you cut out from your egg and attach to the egg by means of nylon thread as described in Talk 8 (page 84). Into the egg also slot the following flannelgraph or Teazlegraph visual aids that can be pulled out: a small chicken, a handkerchief with a blot on it and one without a blot on it, a skull and a cross.

PRESENTATION

Ask children at the service whether they had an Easter egg for Easter. Ask whether any of them had Easter eggs with something inside them. Explain that today we are going to think about God's Easter egg and reveal the egg. What do we find in it?

1. *Death defeated*

Reveal these words. Pull out the skull and place across it the cross. Explain how Christ's death and resurrection defeated death. Our weekly Christian worship on Sundays is a reminder that Christ rose from the dead on the first day of the week victorious over death. Yet despite this weekly reminder most people (including many Christians) do not know that death is defeated (refer to 2 Timothy 1:10 and the Easter proper preface in the *Book of Common Prayer* and *ASB*).

2. *Sinners saved*

Pull out handkerchief with blot on it. This is a picture of any life. All of us are sinners, but Jesus died to take away sin. How do we know that sinners can be saved? The resurrection is the proof that Jesus died for our sins. Refer to 1 John 1:7 and Isaiah 44:22–23. Pull out the other handkerchief that is clean.

3. *Life loosed*

Produce chicken and refer to new life and how, when Jesus rose from the dead and came out of the tomb, life was loosed. He would never die again and those who trust him as their Saviour can receive new life and need not fear physical death, for he has conquered it.

Michael Botting
Editor

24   Easter (3) Five Witnesses

Text

Luke 24:11.

AIM

To show that the disciples in their day doubted the reality of the Resurrection, as many do today. But we know that Jesus is alive.

PREPARATION

Cut out five simple outline figures of people large enough for all to see. Mount them as the talk proceeds on a plain background with the question at the top: 'How can I know that Jesus lives?' One figure will represent man today, and the other four should have long robes so as to represent the prophets, Jesus, the women, the disciples. Each name can be written and placed on a card below the figure.

PRESENTATION

Dead people don't come alive again! No wonder people today doubt the reality of the story of Easter. They did even in Jesus' own day. The disciples were very slow to believe despite all the evidence supporting the fact of the Resurrection. Judge for yourself.

1. The prophets

John 20:9—note 'must rise'! Jesus *had* to come alive again; no other end to the story of his life was possible. Peter, preaching in Jerusalem some weeks later, made the same point: it was 'not possible' for Jesus to remain dead (Acts 2:24). So the Scriptures declared (as foretold by the prophets) that Jesus *must* rise: but still the disciples did not believe. 'How dull you are,' said Jesus. 'How slow to believe all that the prophets have spoken' (Luke 24:25). Jesus *had* to rise, but people refused to believe it.

2. Jesus' words

Jesus said he *would* rise again (Mark 8:31; 9:31; 10:32–34). Three times at least Jesus said he would rise again! What could be clearer than that? But again there were those who either did not understand (Mark 9:32) or just refused to believe it (Matthew 16:22).

3. The women

They came to the tomb and found the stone rolled away. They saw the angels. They remembered Jesus' words. They saw the tomb empty. They ran to tell the disciples. Do you think they believed them? No. Luke 24:11—the Greek word used here by Luke is a medical word for the babblings of a delirious person! They would not believe (Mark 16:11).

4. The disciples

Reports came to them that Jesus was alive. Two had *seen* Jesus alive and talked with him on the road to Emmaus. Peter had seen him. Now it was evening, and the disciples were gathered behind locked doors. But Thomas was not with them. Then as they spoke with the breathless disciples just come back from Emmaus, Jesus appeared before their very eyes! 'We've seen him,' they later told Thomas. 'I don't believe it,' he retorted. 'I tell you, we've *seen* him,' replied another. 'I don't believe it! Unless I see...I will not believe!' (John 20:25). Again, one who doubted. How slow they were to believe, despite all the evidence.

Conclusion

The prophets said he *had* to rise. Jesus said he *would* rise. The women said he *has* risen. The disciples said, 'We've *seen* him!' Later, more than 500 people all at once saw him! Did Jesus really come alive again? Well, what do *you* say? (Produce the last of the five outline figures.) Judge for yourself! If the evidence is so strong, why not trust him and entrust yourself to him? How can I *know* that Jesus is alive? One chorus asks the same question, and gives the answer, 'He lives within my heart.' Can you say that? Obviously, he only lives in the hearts of those who receive him. Have you?

Stephen Trapnell
Marlborough

25   Easter (4) Lord of Life and Death

TEXTS

1 Kings 17:17 to end; John 11: 17−27 (Readings, Easter 3, *ASB*, year 2).

AIM

To explore the full meaning of Jesus' resurrection.

PREPARATION

Make cards for Teazlegraph with 'toration', 'uscitation' and 'urrection' on them, plus larger card with 'Res' on it to go in front of the other cards. Also cut out of bright coloured paper a skull, a tombstone and Jesus' empty tomb, as shown below.

Ask congregation if they have been listening carefully to the two readings, and if they can tell you the link. (Bringing someone back from the dead.)

Put card with 'Res' up on board.

Ask what word beginning 'res' is at the heart of this wonderful story about the prophet Elijah. You will probably get 'resurrection'—if so ask again until the correct answer 'restoration' is given. Talk about the horror felt by the widow as her child got worse and worse. Put up the skull. Death was staring her in the face. How fearful she must have felt. First she lost her husband and now she was going to lose her only son. But Elijah takes the boy and, full of indignation against God, prays for God to restore the boy to life. And God does so.

Refer to similar story of Elisha and the Shunamite widow's son—the way the prophet placed himself over the boy, and the boy's sneezes as he revived, are reckoned by some medical authorities to indicate mouth to mouth resuscitation. If so, this instance is the first ever recorded!

Elijah wondered how God could do such a terrible thing to this poor widow who had been so kind to him. But God showed that he *does* care. Quote Matthew 10:29, 'Are not two sparrows sold for a penny? Yet not one of them will fall to the ground apart from the will of your Father.' God *is* in control. We must have faith. God's power is stronger than anything in all creation. 'Perfect love casts out fear.' God is Lord of *all* of life, and this gives us hope.

Lazarus' story is about a word we've already mentioned (Resuscitation) because unlike the widow's son there was no doubt that Lazarus was well and truly dead. Put up tombstone.

Retell main points of the story. Jesus waited two days; Lazarus had been dead for four days; Martha's objection to opening the tomb; Jesus commands Lazarus to come out and he does so still trailing the winding sheet.

Jesus' command reaches beyond the grave: his words were

heard by a dead man! Quote, Jesus said, 'I am the resurrection and the life.'

The power and the fear of death are broken. Bringing someone back from the dead is impossible, but 'All things are possible with God' (Mark 10:27).

Those who do not know Jesus are still dead in their sins. But Jesus still speaks to the dead. 'For while we were yet sinners, Christ died for us.' Jesus is Lord over life and death. Belief in Jesus as the Resurrection brings a new start.

Easter is all about Res-urrection. Jesus has come back to life like Lazarus did, in so far as Jesus was well and truly dead. Remind congregation of how the soldiers made sure that this was so. But in contrast to Lazarus who eventually died again (presumably of old age), Jesus was raised *never to die again*. Put up picture of empty tomb.

'For we know that since Christ was raised from the dead, he cannot die again: death no longer has mastery over him' (Romans 6:9).

Talk about spiritual death as opposed to physical death. 'Whoever lives and believes in me shall never die' (John 11:26).

Full meaning of 'Immanuel'—God with us—Jesus is with us for all eternity. 'By his power God raised the Lord from the dead, and he will raise us also' (1 Corinthians 6:14).

Jesus is Lord—the giver of life.

Conclude by quoting 1 Corinthians 15:58: 'Give yourselves fully to the work of the Lord, because you know that your labour in the Lord is not in vain.' Explain that *because* we know that one day we shall share Jesus' resurrection all we do now to try to be good disciples of Jesus will be worth while—nothing will be wasted.

David McIntosh
Ellesmere Port

26   Easter (5) An Easter Present

TEXT

Mark 16:3.

AIM

To show that the emptiness of the tomb was very important.

PREPARATION

The visual aid is based on a large empty cardboard box, with two flaps as the lid at the top. These are each painted white, with the words 'Don't be alarmed, you are looking for Jesus who was crucified' on one, and the words 'He has risen, he is not here. See the place where they laid him.' on the other flap. Inside the box are some linen bandages. On the side of the box is written 'Happy Easter' in large print, and the box appears to be firmly tied together with string to prevent anyone easily opening it but (as it will appear in section 2) the string does not prevent the flaps being opened, so to achieve this effect they will need to be taped at the top and hidden from the congregation.

It's Easter today. Is it going to be a happy Easter or an unhappy Easter? Maybe this box or present will help us.

1. The first Easter was not very happy for the early disciples, for their Lord Jesus had been crucified, dead and buried and they expected him to stay dead. So they went to the tomb to complete the embalming process and wrapping of the dead body of Jesus. However they found an Easter present, just as we have today.

2. Now this Easter present is tied up with some very tough string, and however much I try I don't think I will be able to get the knots undone and find out what is inside this box. I certainly would not be able to break this string with my bare hands. Who is going to help open this Easter present? Do you remember what the women said as they went to the tomb? 'Who will roll the stone away from the entrance of the tomb?' But if I look at the top of this box the string actually doesn't prevent the flaps being opened; just as when the women went to the tomb, they found that the stone had already been rolled away from the entrance.

3. Ah! Now it's open, we can get inside, and look to see what's there. Oh, how disappointing! Nothing valuable—just a bit of wrapping inside. Remind children that sometimes valuable birthday presents come with a lot of packing or wrapping. I expected a really lovely present but there's nothing inside. Actually, this is what the first women saw; the tomb was empty. It was not what they were expecting—and so they asked themselves 'What does this mean?'

4. Now the women saw two angels outside: there are two flaps on this box representing the two angels. I have written down what the angels said. 'Don't be alarmed, you are looking for Jesus who was crucified' and 'He has risen, he is not here. See the place where they laid him.'

5. Now there is something at the bottom of this box if I reach right down. It's some white linen bandages. This reminds me that the tomb wasn't actually empty. Although the

body of Jesus wasn't there, the bandages were still there. This means that thieves did not steal the body, because the valuable ointments were left in the bandages. Thieves would have taken everything. Also, as in John's gospel, the bandages were in two separate neat piles, as if they still contained the body! The body was not there, but it proved to the disciples that instead of someone unwrapping the body and smuggling it away, the body of Jesus moved through the bandages in the Resurrection, just as later he moved through closed doors to meet the disciples.

6. The Resurrection really did happen! So it turned out to be a happy Easter after all—for them and for us.

David Williams
Cheltenham

27   Ascension (1) The Benefits

Text

John 16:7.

Aim

To show that we are better off today since Jesus has ascended and the Holy Spirit has come.

Preparation

Write the figures '40' and '50' on two cards. Cut out six simple outlines of men at least 12″ high, in two contrasting colours, three of each. These are to represent Jesus and the Spirit of Jesus. Prepare ten large bold arrows in cardboard of simple design:

$$\triangleright \; \bigcirc$$

Back each of the figures and arrows with self-adhesive materials, or punch with a hole and hang on pins placed in the board beforehand. Arrange the visual aid so to build up as follows:

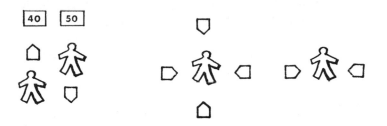

Place the cards marked 40 and 50 on the board. Explain the timing of Ascension (40 days after Easter) and Pentecost (50 days after). Ascension was the end of Jesus' public ministry on earth. The disciples saw Jesus disappear into a cloud as he was taken up from them. (Place silhouette of Jesus on board with an arrow pointing upwards.) You might say that Jesus being taken from them was the worst thing that could happen, for they lost thereby the best friend they ever had. But no! Jesus told his disciples that it was *to their advantage* that he left them, for his going away would enable the Holy Spirit to come. (Place the silhouette of the Spirit of Jesus on the board with an arrow pointing down.) We tend to envy the disciples who were with Jesus on earth, listening to his preaching, seeing his miracles, enjoying the sheer delight of just being with him. Surely, we say, they were better off to be with Jesus in their day, than we are nearly 2000 years later. But no! Jesus said that those who are his disciples today (i.e. those who have received him by faith and are his followers) have every advantage, because we have the Holy Spirit, the Spirit of Jesus, with us. You don't believe it?

1. (Take the second figure of Jesus and point the four arrows towards it.) In the time of Jesus' ministry on earth, if you wanted to meet Jesus, *you had to go to him*. This is exactly what happened: once people knew of his whereabouts, they

came to him from every quarter. (Now superimpose the figure of the Spirit of Jesus on top of Jesus.) But when the Holy Spirit comes, we don't have to go to the Holy Land to meet with Jesus: *he comes to us*, wherever we are (turn the arrows round, so they all point outwards). Whereas long ago Jesus was necessarily confined to one particular place, since he ascended and the Holy Spirit descended he is present everywhere. *He comes to us.* This is obviously to our advantage.

2. What is true in the realm of space is also true in the matter of time. (Place another figure of Jesus on the board, with arrows either side pointing towards him.) Jesus began his ministry in about the year AD 25, and his ministry lasted for about three years, so far as we know.

Now if you or I wanted to meet with Jesus, we would have to have lived in the same era: that is to say, we would have to have been first-century disciples living in the late AD 20s. But when Jesus ascended and the Holy Spirit descended (superimpose the figure of the Spirit of Jesus on top of that of Jesus) people in every age could draw near to Christ. (Change the two arrows so that they point outwards; and add two more beyond the one pointing to the right, representing 'for all time'.)

Conclusion

We have the Spirit of Jesus with us for ever: from one generation to another. This is also to our great advantage. The Ascension of Jesus and the coming of the Holy Spirit mean that we are much better off today than the disciples were in their day; we have the presence of Jesus with us *everywhere, and for all time*.

Stephen Trapnell
Marlborough

28   Ascension (2) Three Letters

Acts 1:6–11.

AIM

To teach what happened on the day Jesus returned to heaven.

PREPARATION

Prepare three giant envelopes and contents as follows:
1.   A birthday letter.
2.   A royal letter.
3.   A private letter.

PRESENTATION

Introduction

Goodbyes are sad events, e.g. after a wonderful holiday, at the beginning of a new term. The day came when Jesus had to say goodbye to his friends. He had been with them for three years and more. He had died for them, and he had been alive with them for forty days. He led them out to Bethany, a little village two miles outside Jerusalem. And his last words to them were rather like very special letters.

147

Envelope 1:
John Smith,
St. Paul's Church,
Climbing.

The Bank of Heaven: Anytime
Pay: All Christians
Sum: 'You shall   £Acts 1:8
receive power'   Jesus Christ

O.H.M.S.

John Smith,
St. Paul's Church,
Climbing.

'Be my
witnesses'
Acts 1 v 8

Private

John Smith,
St. Paul's Church,
Climbing.

'This Jesus....
will come'
Acts 1 v 11

1. *The first letter*

This letter begins with the letter B; can you guess what kind
of a letter it is? A birthday letter (show). Birthday letters
often have presents inside, and this letter is no exception.
This first message of Jesus spoke of a birthday gift.

(Show and open birthday letter.) Turn with me to the
words of Jesus in Acts 1:8, 'You shall receive power.' How
and when? 'When the Holy Spirit has come upon you.'
While Jesus was living on earth he couldn't be everywhere
at once! So when he returned triumphantly into heaven,
back to his Father, he sent his Holy Spirit to be with
everyone who trusted him. It was, and still is, just as
though Jesus was with us. When we receive a birthday

present, we accept it and thank the giver. So with this gift, promised by the Lord Jesus. We thank him for coming to this earth and living here and then dying for us and then coming alive again on the first Easter Day, and returning to his Father in heaven. When we thank him for doing this and believe this promise of his to send his Holy Spirit to be with us, then he *will* be with us.

Recap: So the first message on the day Jesus went back to heaven was that there was a gift to accept. What a gift!

2. *The second letter*

The second message is like another letter—a letter with these four initials on the envelope: OHMS. Can anyone tell me what they stand for? On Her Majesty's Service. Here is a command to obey! (E.g. letter demanding Income Tax.)

Look at verse 8 again, for there is a command to obey. Can you see it? (Show.) 'Be my witnesses.' What is a witness? (Give relevant example.)

In the same way, as witnesses to the Lord Jesus, we obey this command by showing others what he is like. Now those first witnesses had seen him with their eyes, and so their witness was special and unique. Yet we too can be witnesses by pointing to the Jesus we see in the Bible, and by pointing to the Jesus we know in our lives.

3. *The third letter*

Back to that hill near Bethany! As his friends were talking with Jesus, they suddenly saw that a cloud had come between them and him, and his feet were no longer touching the ground. He was lifted up into the cloud and they saw him no more! The third message did not come from Jesus, but from two angels who were standing there—two men in white clothes. This message is like a third letter—a letter beginning with P. A private letter (show). We read the message in verse 11: 'This Jesus...will come' (show). I have called it a private letter, because it was one that only those who loved and believed in the Lord Jesus would believe and accept. The secret was and is that Jesus is coming again! Do you believe that? A wonderful promise to believe and to share with all those who trust him.

Summary

Goodbyes are often sad events, but the day Jesus went back to heaven was not sad in the same way because of the three wonderful messages given to us:

One like a birthday letter, a gift to accept, his Holy Spirit.

One like a King's command, be my witnesses.

One like a private secret, he is coming again!

So we look forward to that day when he will return, and until then we accept his gift, obey his command and believe the secret.

Garry Guinness
Worthing

29   Ascension (3) Hope

TEXT

Matthew 28:16–end.

AIM

To show how the Ascension gives hope for the present and future.

PREPARATION

Cut out figures to represent people, with a larger one for Jesus, coloured, say, green on one side and yellow on the reverse.

Make a symbol to represent God, e.g. .

Make a cross with room for lettering.

Make two arrows marked and .

PRESENTATION

1. Talk about everyday life and people on earth, putting up the smaller figures.
2. Talk about God, who lives in heaven, and about our ideas of him, putting up your symbol for God.
3. Talk about the incarnation, and how God came to earth,

putting the 'CAME' arrow pointing between God and the people.

4. Talk about what happened to Jesus and how he was put to death on the cross, putting the figure of Jesus on the cross. Then describe how Jesus passed through death and was raised to new life, reversing the figure and putting it on the other side of the cross.

5. Now Jesus invites us to follow him, and offers us new life through faith. Add the word COME to the cross bar of the cross, and reverse some of the people and put them on the other side of the cross.

6. Describe the Ascension and the reasons for it, moving the Jesus figure and putting it inside the circle with the God symbol.

7. Talk about the fact that we now have hope for the present and the future because Jesus has been raised from the dead and has ascended into heaven. Add the 'HOPE' arrow pointing from the reversed people towards God.

Judith Rose
Rochester

30   The Whitsun Windmill

TEXT

2 Corinthians 6:1.
(Suggested readings: John 3:1−8 or 2 Corinthians 6:1−10.)

AIM

To show how Christians should be workers with God and each other in the power of the Holy Spirit.

PREPARATION

Cut the shape of a windmill out of two pieces of cardboard. In the front one make two doors which when you open them reveal pictures of the miller and of Jesus (which are in fact stuck on the back one). The sails are made separately out of two long pieces of cardboard which cross in the middle and are attached to the windmill by a split-pin so that they will go round if you twist them. Prepare four pieces of card the same size as each of the four sails and write on them: 'workers', 'together', 'with', 'God'; these can be attached to the sails either by double-sided sellotape or by having pieces of elastic round the sails at either end and in the middle so that the words will tuck in.

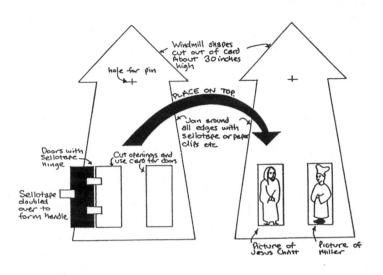

Windmill shapes cut out of card About 30 inches high

hole for pin

PLACE ON TOP.

Join around all edges with sellotape or paper clips etc.

Doors with Sellotape hinge

Cut openings and use card for doors

Sellotape doubled over to form handle

Picture of Jesus Christ

Picture of Miller

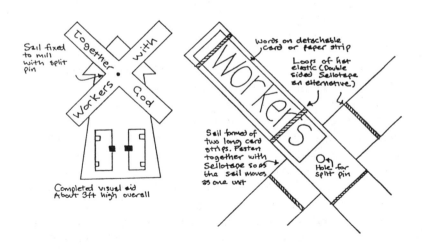

Sail fixed to mill with split pin

together with Workers God

Completed visual aid About 3ft high overall

Words on detachable card or paper strip

Loops of hat elastic (Double sided Sellotape an alternative.)

Workers

Sail formed of two long card strips. Fasten together with Sellotape so as the sail moves as one unit

Hole for split pin

Explain how when Jesus was on earth he went around the countryside and told stories about sheep, corn, etc to tell us about God and the kingdom of heaven. Then produce the windmill without the words and say how we can learn about God from it. This windmill works; show them that the sails will go round when you twist them. Say that your sails help the miller to make flour and put 'workers' on the first sail. Explain that we are supposed to work for God too. We can do this in many ways: by doing good deeds, helping the sick, the poor, the lonely, the deprived, by finding others who have not heard about Jesus to tell of what he means to us, or by carrying out various jobs to help others from day to day. Explain that the power that makes the windmill work is the wind, and liken this to God's Holy Spirit.

Point out that the sails go round together (put up 'together') and that Christians are supposed to work together too. In other words we are not to serve God on our own but with others. Suggest that the traffic is like this. If all the cars decided they would travel on whichever side of the road they fancied we would have chaos and crashes. So they all go in the same direction. So Christians must work together to achieve order and purpose in the Christian church.

Whom do the sails work for? Show the picture of the miller and say that we are to work for God as the sails work for the miller. Show the picture of Jesus. In conclusion, show that the sails can do nothing unless the miller is also working inside and add 'with God' on the last two sails as you explain that Christians also have to work with God and our efforts without God are of no use. Just as the sails going round are no use unless the miller has put corn there to be worked on to be ground into flour, so our efforts without God working with us and us with God are of no use.

A Bible story to show how we can work with God is the story of Paul and his journey to Macedonia after he had been given a dream by God of the man asking him to come over to help them. He obeyed God's call and so worked with God.

Use the idea of different sails working together to explain how we are all part of the Christian church but each part is different and yet all work together in the same body, the church. Paul alludes to this in 1 Corinthians 12 where he talks about the different parts of the body having different functions but all being part of the one body.

Christopher Porteous
Beckenham

31 Pentecost and You

TEXTS

Acts 2:1–4 and Ephesians 5:18.

AIM

To help people understand what it is to be filled with the Spirit and to keep being filled with the Spirit.

PREPARATION

You will need a selection of various sizes and types of jug and teapot:
1. A jug.
2. Three jugs—china jug, translucent plastic jug and clear glass jug, each almost filled with orange juice.
3. Three teapots—one average sized one, one small individual one and one huge 'Women's Fellowship' type teapot.

PRESENTATION

I wonder what it means to be filled with the Spirit. Let's use a few illustrations to help us to understand.
1. (Show an inverted jug to everyone.) This jug is inverted, and isn't much use to anyone. It can't be used for the purpose for which it was designed, and the maker cannot

use it at the moment. This jug needs to be turned the other way up; it needs to be turned the right way up. In other words it needs to be 'con-verted' so that it is the right way up and can be used. Now that it is con-verted properly it can be filled and used.

2. I have three different types of jug here, each of which has been con-verted and can be filled and used. This china jug is filled, but you can't tell if it's filled until you get very close to it and look inside it. Then you can decide whether you want to have the drink that is in this jug. Now there are some Christians who are secret Christians and you have to get very close to them to be able to see what is inside them.

This next jug is a translucent plastic jug, and you can tell that there is something in it but you can't tell exactly what it is. There is something there, and perhaps you think it's worthwhile going up close to look inside to decide whether you want what's inside or not.

The third jug is a glass jug and everyone can see what's inside it. If you want, in this case orange to drink, you will go up to it to have your glass filled.

3. Let's look at these teapots now. Teapots are all very useful but there are different sizes. We have got this usual family teapot here which is quite good for a few people and this could be filled with tea before it's used for pouring out. Of course, the lid has to be taken off before it can be filled. It makes you think about whether you have to take your lid off, so to speak, to let God fill you with his Spirit. Is there any barrier in your life to stop the Master filling you with his Spirit?

I now have this miniature teapot which is only enough for one person, but it can still be filled! This can still be filled one hundred per cent, just as much as the bigger teapot can be filled one hundred per cent. It doesn't matter how small you think you are to God, you can still be filled with his Holy Spirit!

I have also got this huge catering teapot here, and this also can be filled and the Master can use it for filling up lots and lots of teacups from other people. Like the other teapots the lid still has to come off before it can be used for pouring itself out to other people.

4. A final point could be that when these jugs and teapots have been poured out in the service of other people they become empty and drained. Have you ever felt that in Christian service? What needs to happen, of course, is that they should go back and be refilled and then again used in the Master's service.

David Williams
Cheltenham

32   Pentecost—Wind, Tongues and Fire

TEXT

Acts 2:1–4 (or possibly to verse 21).

AIM

To give a simple explanation of the coming of the Holy Spirit to the church on the Day of Pentecost.

PREPARATION

Have a whistle, a pair of fire bellows and a recording on cassette of a foreign language being spoken.

PRESENTATION

Assuming the talk is being given on Whitsunday (Pentecost), ask what day it is. What do we often receive on special days, like Christmas or birthdays? On obtaining the answer of presents, ask what present the disciples received that day.

What do we mean by the Holy Spirit? Let us see what we can learn from the Lesson we heard this morning (assuming that the text above and further verses were read).

1. Tongues

Play the recording of the foreign language. Ask if anyone can understand it. Possibly someone might, whereas others may know the language, even if they cannot translate. Read verse 4 of text. Clearly a miracle was taking place, for the disciples could probably only speak Aramaic and Greek, yet the crowds gathered in Jerusalem for the festival were hearing them speak in a wide variety of languages, depending on where they were born.

Ask whether we should refer to the Holy Spirit as 'he' or 'it'. Draw out that he must be a Person, because things don't speak. If challenged, point out that tape-recorders and radios etc are reproducing *people's* voices.

Explain that the Holy Spirit is the third Person of the Holy Trinity that we refer to when saying the Creed and the Grace (2 Corinthians 13:14). It was very important that he helped the disciples to speak, because they, and we today, are told to use the gift of speech to worship God (Acts 2:11) and to witness to the Lord Jesus (Acts 1:8).

2. Sound

Blow the whistle. What are you hearing? Explain that they were hearing the sound of wind and it was the sound of wind that those first disciples heard. Explain that that was very appropriate for the coming of the Spirit, because the Spirit is very like a wind. Indeed in Greek the words for wind, breath and spirit are all the same word—*pneuma*, from which we get words like 'pneumatic', which we use to describe a drill that works by wind, or a tyre filled with air. Neither the wind nor Spirit can be seen, but we often know they are there by the sound. Peter preached to the crowds, but it was more than Peter speaking, for they also heard the inner voice of the Holy Spirit speaking, leading them to repent and believe.

3. Fire

Produce fire bellows and ask what they are. Explain that in places where it is legal to have coal fires they can help a fire to burn more brightly. Obviously the tongues of fire that fell on the disciples were unique, but it was a very appropriate sign because John the Baptist had said earlier that Jesus would baptise with the Holy Spirit and with fire (Luke 3:16). That is what the disciples were experiencing. It changed their lives and led them to preach boldly about the need to turn from sin, to trust in the Lord Jesus Christ for salvation, to receive the Holy Spirit and to lead holy lives.

A boy I used to teach at a boarding preparatory school, suddenly changed for the better, and began reading his Bible and praying before he went to bed. On enquiry it turned out that the change came after a church service the entire school had attended. Others had heard the same sermon, but it had not had any particular effect. This boy had heard not just the preacher, but the voice of God the Holy Spirit, and we all knew because we saw the change in his life. (Either adapt this story or use a similar one from your own experience.)

Might the same Holy Spirit be speaking in that way to some here this morning? Then you should respond by repenting of your sins, trusting in Jesus for salvation and receive the special gift of the Holy Spirit that those disciples received on the very first Whitsunday.

Michael Botting
Editor

33   The Trinity (1)

To show that the doctrine of the Trinity is not so confusing as it appears, once you know Christ.

PREPARATION

1. Prepare or obtain a large plan of some complicated road intersection in your locality or in recent news (e.g. Spaghetti Junction).

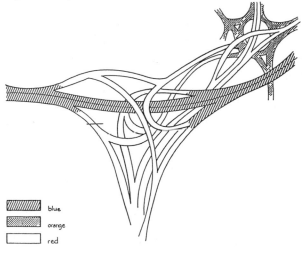

blue

orange

red

163

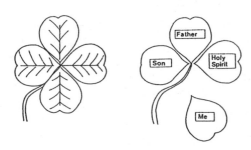

2. Prepare two cards or strips of paper with **TRI** and **UNITY** overlapping to give **TRINITY**.
3. Draw on paper or on acetate sheet (for overhead projector) a clover-leaf crossing.
4. Try to get one of the children beforehand to find a four-leaf clover to show. Draw a large four-leaf clover to fit over the crossing.
5. Prepare cards (or acetates) with 'Father', 'Son', 'Holy Spirit' and 'me' to go on separate clover leaves of the same size.
6. Prepare cards (acetates)—'know', 'look', 'go'.

PRESENTATION

Show picture of road intersection. What is this? Confusing, isn't it? But it is not so bad if you are actually involved in it, driving through it, provided that you *know* where you want to go, *look* at the instructions—or the friend in the car ahead who is showing you the way—and *go* ahead.

If it is Trinity Sunday or season ask, 'What is today called in the church year?' What is the Trinity? It means God the Father, God the Son and God the Holy Spirit. Confused? You need not be if you are involved.

Here is another road junction—a clover-leaf crossing, based on the shape of a four-leaf clover. Ever seen one? Could not find a four-leaf clover—here is a three-leaf clover, one leaf yet three leaves. Three in one. Just like the Trinity. The Trinity is really two words put together, TRI and UNITY.

In the Old Testament the writers make it clear that Jews believed in *one* God (UNITY) (Deuteronomy 6:4). When Jesus came and claimed to be God the Son, the Jews were confused and offended and tried to kill him for blasphemy (John 8:58,59). The apostles gradually believed that Jesus was God (Matthew 16:16; John 20:28). When God the Holy Spirit fell on them at Pentecost, they would have been even more confused if Jesus had not warned them in advance (Acts 1:4). They were involved—confusion was banished as they experienced the Tri-unity—three persons but one God; three aspects of the one divine Being; God in action as Creator (Father), Saviour (Son) and Helper (Holy Spirit). The fourth leaf is you or me. When you accept God the Son, Jesus, as your Saviour, God the Father adopts you into his family and gives you God the Holy Spirit to make you more like Jesus.

Thus the Trinity is less confusing once you are involved in it—
Know where you want to go—heaven, the Father's home
Look how the way has been made for us—by Jesus (John 14:6)
Go ahead in the power of the Holy Spirit.

Conclusion

God wants us to be united with him, and then we will come to understand more and more of his character as Father, Son and Holy Spirit.

Peter Barton
Malmesbury

34 The Trinity (2)

TEXT

2 Corinthians 13:14 (verse 13 in the Good News Bible).

AIM

To gain understanding of some of the mysteries of the Trinity.

PREPARATION

Cut out a number of equilateral triangles (i.e. with sides of equal length—for instance 10″) of the same size in card. Use four to sellotape one triangle to each of the sides of a central triangle (so that they could fold away, or fold upwards to a point). Use another four to make a permanent 'triangular pyramid' (i.e. a tetrahedron): on this put the word 'God' on one face and either the words (or their initials) on the other three faces: Father, Son, Holy Spirit. Also, get a child's tricycle, a photographer's tripod and perhaps a picture of the local community centre. Write on two lengths of card the words 'Tricycle' (folding the card so that initially only the letters TRI can be seen) and 'Community' (folding the card so that initially only the letters NITY can be seen).

Today is Trinity Sunday. Have you ever wondered what the word 'Trinity' means? You may have heard us talk about 'God the Father', 'Jesus' and 'the Holy Spirit'. But are they one God or three? What a mystery! Look at these two cards which I am holding together to spell the word TRINITY. This strange word has bits of two familiar words; let me explain. (Either pick up the tricycle, or perhaps get a child to ride up the aisle to you.) Why is it called a *tri*cycle? (Three wheels—balance, safety, movement.) Pick up the tripod. Why and what is it used for? (Stability on any surface, etc.) Show picture of community centre. What is it? It means a unity people have in common: a common-unity, or a 'community' centre—it's about people getting on well together. Putting these two words together, we have the word TRINITY.

Now let's try and make some models. I've got here some triangles. Why is it called a triangle? It has three angles and three sides. Can you tell me something about all the three angles/sides? (All the same.) Now let me hold this one upright. Can you point to the top? If I move it round (i.e. till the next point is at the top)—is it the same, or the one now at the top? Are you puzzled? But really it's quite simple. Now do you get some idea of how simple, and yet how puzzling the Trinity of God is?

So let's get on to an actual model. (Try assembling some, and failing—this usually revives attention!) Well, I've got one ready made up: a triangular pyramid—or a tetrahedron for the clever ones at school. I've written God's name on the different sides. On the base: GOD; on the three sloping sides: FATHER, SON, and HOLY SPIRIT. How does this work?

(Show base: GOD.) Sometimes in the Bible or our prayers we just think of God. Well, that's true—nothing wrong with that. (Show side FATHER.) Sometimes we just think of Father in our prayers or (show side JESUS) the wonderful person in the gospel stories or (show side HOLY SPIRIT) the gracious power of the Spirit at Pentecost. But each one is truly

God (for each person, turn the face over to show the word GOD).

Also, sometimes we read of the Son, Jesus, praying to the Father (rotate tetrahedron to display first the side Father to the congregation, then the side Jesus). Both are equally God.

At the Baptism, or the prayer we shall have at the end of the service (i.e. the grace) we think of our one God as all three: Father, Son and Holy Spirit (rotate the three faces, with the apex facing the congregation) but each one is equally God (show base). As with this model, I can't tell you which is the top, or the most important person, or the least important. Each is equally God: there is only one God (one model) but each person has a different work in the unity of the Trinity.

Conclusion

The Trinity may seem a mystery, but it is also a great joy. Enjoy the security of the heavenly Father, enjoy salvation with the Saviour Jesus and enjoy the strength of the Spirit.

David Williams
Cheltenham

35   Harvest (1) Wheat and Weeds

Matthew 13:24–30, 36–43.

AIM

To help people see the need to accept Christ as Saviour before it is too late.

PREPARATION

Wheat and tares

Dr Plumptre, writing in Ellicott's *Bible Commentary for English Readers*, relates that the act of an enemy sowing tares among wheat

> was then—and still is—a common form of Eastern malice or revenge. It easily escaped detection. It inflicted both loss and trouble. The 'enemy' had the satisfaction of brooding for weeks or months over the prospect of the injury he had inflicted, and the vexation it would cause when discovered. The tares, known to botanists as the *Lolium temulentum*, or *darnel*, grew up at first with stalk and blade like the wheat; it was not till fructification began that the difference was easily detected. It adds to the point of the parable to remember that the seeds of the tares were not merely useless as food, but were positively noxious.

This is really the main point of the parable, namely, that just as wheat and tares initially look very much alike, so to begin with can those who have accepted Jesus Christ as their Saviour and those who have not. Therefore, we who profess and call ourselves Christians must not be too quick to judge one another—that is solely God's prerogative. Our primary task as teachers of the word of God is to lead our people to a saving knowledge of Christ or, in the language of the farmer, to sow seeds in our people's hearts that will bring forth fruit to eternal life. We ourselves shall frequently not be at all sure, perhaps for some time, which people have really responded to God's word, but fortunately we are not judged by our success but by our faithfulness in teaching what he has told us. The parable under consideration here brings especial need for honesty and faithfulness, for it undoubtedly teaches the fact of both heaven and hell.

God's love and justice

The twin doctrines of God's love for sinners and his judgement on sin must not be separated. The Bible clearly teaches both. For us to accept one and reject the other means that we really deny the Bible as our ultimate authority, and, if we do that, we cannot really be sure even of God's love. In fact, there is no antagonism between his love and his justice. They both met at Calvary, where we see demonstrated God's love for us sinners and his judgement on our sins. In this lesson, therefore, we must make clear that those who persist in sin and refuse God's loving offer of salvation will one day be judged and, like the tares, destroyed. The point to stress, however, is that if this should happen it is our fault—not God's. Hell was never prepared for man but for the devil and his angels (cf Matthew 25:34, 41).

'Those who are tares today may be wheat tomorrow' (St Augustine).

Visual aid

Prepare seven pieces of cardboard folded in the middle horizontally, with the following words:

on the top half:

Farmer   Field   Wheat   Enemy   Tares   Harvest   Barn

on the bottom half:

Jesus   World   Saved   Devil   Lost   End-of-World   Heaven

It is helpful if the words 'Farmer', 'Wheat' and 'Barn' are printed on a yellow background, 'Enemy' and 'Tares' on a red background, 'Field' on green and 'Harvest' on orange. The actual lettering for 'Farmer', 'Wheat' and 'Barn' could be printed in green and the lettering of 'Jesus', 'Saved' and 'Heaven' printed in red. All other lettering should be black.

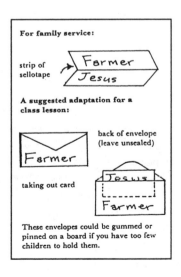

The fold in the cards should be made by cutting the front with a sharp, single-edged razor blade, the pressure being insufficient to cut right through the card. It is wise also to put a strip of sellotape along the back of the fold.

Before the service

Before the Harvest Service, select seven children whom you can rely on, say, five boys and two girls, and distribute the cards among them, the girls holding 'Field' and 'Harvest'. Tell them to come up to the front immediately before your talk and sit on seven chairs you have placed in front for the purpose. Tell the children that when they hear you mention in your talk the word on the top of their card they should stand up and show the top of their card to everyone else, keeping the lower half bent back so that it is out of view. During the second part of your talk the children should bend the lower part of their card down, when the word on it has been guessed by the other children listening. Mention also to the children holding 'Field', 'Enemy', 'Tares' and 'Harvest' to be ready to sit down just before your talk ends, when you indicate.

PRESENTATION

Jesus often liked to tell stories to the people. He would perhaps be sitting in a boat by the seaside with the people on the beach. One day he caught sight of a sower sowing his seed on a hillside (point to an imaginary sower in the distance), and so he used this as the subject for a story. Of course, Jesus was rather like a sower himself, sowing seeds of ideas into people's minds and hearts. That will also happen today, as I tell you one of his stories. Let us pray that the seeds that fall into our minds and hearts now may grow and bring forth fruit to eternal life. (Short prayer.)

Wheat and tares

Tell as vividly as you can the parable of the tares among the wheat, emphasising that wheat and tares look alike in the early days of growth. Your retelling of the parable will be more effective if you have read the story many times over yourself beforehand and then retold it to yourself aloud without notes. Added effect can be given (say) by rubbing your hands together as you imagine the enemy gloating over what he has done as he thinks about the tares growing up without the farmer knowing. As you tell the story, be sure to mention in order the seven words on the top of your cards and glance towards the children helping you to ensure that each stands up at the right moment.

Disciples question Jesus

Having told the story, mention how Jesus told other stories and then sent the people away. The disciples of Jesus, however, later gathered round him and asked him to explain the parable, which he did. Now throw the interpretation of the parable to the children by asking them to explain it for you.

'Who do you think the farmer was?' (Mention that you have already given them a hint, for before your prayer you should have said that Jesus was like a sower.) Having received the answer that the Farmer is Jesus, see that the boy holding the card bends down the lower part to reveal the word Jesus on it. Proceed now to draw from the other children that the Field is the World and get the lower part of that card displayed.

Consider now who Jesus' enemy is (i.e. do not deal with Wheat yet). Discuss briefly the great battle that is going on in the world between Jesus and the devil. Something of this battle was seen in Bible days, for example, when Herod killed all the baby boys in Bethlehem at the first Christmas time; the temptation in the wilderness at the beginning of Jesus' ministry; and the temptation to escape the cross in the Garden of Gethsemane. Jesus was completely triumphant, but still the war rages, even though the devil knows he is a defeated enemy. This battle rages in the hearts of boys and girls, men and women.

Those who follow Jesus are called in the parable—what? (Wheat.) Turn down the word Saved. Those who follow the devil are called what? (Tares.) Turn down the word Lost. Explain that just as we saw that Wheat and Tares are difficult to tell apart at first, so are the Saved and Lost. Each of us knows whether we have asked Jesus to be our Saviour from sin and are seeking to make him the Lord of our lives, but we cannot be sure about others. Some of our friends may seem from the outside to be very nice, but what goes on in their hearts may be very different. There may be evil thoughts leading to evil words and deeds that we don't hear or see. So we are not to judge which are which, for we might be wrong. Besides, though the parable does not say so, the rest of Scripture makes clear that there is still time to change and 'those who are tares today may be wheat tomorrow'. You might explain briefly here how to change from being Tares to Wheat, or suggest that those people who want to know should ask you after the service.

However, one day there is going to be a great harvest festival—the greatest harvest festival ever. When will that be? Draw from the children End-of-World and get the girl holding that card to let the lower part down. When that day comes, and we cannot say when it will be, then it will be too late to change. Jesus will send his angel reapers to gather up the Tares, and the Lost will be separated from God for ever. Explain that these are not your words, but the words of the most loving and kind Person who ever lived. It is because he loves us so much that he has warned us this is going to happen. If someone knows that a part of the beach at the seaside is dangerous, it is an act of love and kindness to warn people. Jesus warns us that if we reject him and continue to follow the devil the result will be deadly serious. (Now make Field, Devil, Tares and Harvest sit down.) However, for all who follow Jesus he will gather the Saved into his Barn. Where is that? (Heaven.) Describe briefly what a wonderful place that will be for all who love Jesus Christ.

Michael Botting
Editor

(Note: This talk by Michael Botting has been adapted by kind permission of Scripture Union from the outline first published in *Teaching Juniors*, July–September 1966.)

36   Harvest (2) Christian Cabbages

TEXT

Matthew 13:1–9.

AIM

To show the things which can spoil our Christian lives.

PREPARATION

You need a couple of moth-eaten looking cabbages and a good one. The greengrocer will probably sell you both kinds and they are not wasted if you eat them after the talk.

Or you can draw your cabbages. Make large pictures of a snail, a slug and a caterpillar out of cardboard, and stick black paper over them to make a shadow effect, so that you can stick on letters made out of fluorescent paper. The cabbages are to represent Christians, and the slug is named Sin, the snail Sloth and the caterpillar Self. You will also need a picture of a good gardener who is to represent God, a net to protect the good cabbage which is Trust, and a bottle of insecticide which is Obey. These items can be bought or made out of cardboard. They can be hung on hooks as the talk proceeds, or attached to a Teazlegraph board.

Moth-eaten cabbage   Good cabbage

Use real cabbages or produce pictures. Pictures have the advantage that they may be hung on hooks screwed to a board, or attached to Teazlegraph or flannelgraph. This also applies to other items required for this talk.

Cut shapes out of black card to form silhouettes of snail, slug and caterpillar.

Letters cut out of fluorescent paper and stuck on.

If an actual bottle of insecticide is used, instead of a picture, make a large, clear label for it, which may be easily read at a distance. In fact any large bottle clearly labelled will do.

177

PRESENTATION

Begin by explaining that you are a rotten gardener and that whenever you try to grow things that should look good they are nearly always failures. Produce your two rotten cabbages. Then explain that many Christians are like your rotten cabbages, and only a few are like the good one which you produce. Say that just as things come along to spoil cabbages, so there are things which spoil our Christian lives. Produce in turn the snail, the slug and the caterpillar, and explain their significance. Then explain that God has given us things to help us in our lives just as the gardener has things which help him in his work. God is the good gardener and the net is to protect—it is our trust in God. The insecticide which kills insects is like our obedience to his word.

Christopher Porteous
Beckenham

37 Harvest (3) Fruit

TEXT

Galatians 5:22.

AIM

To show that unless the Lord Jesus is controlling our lives, then there will be no lasting goodness from the things we do.

PREPARATION

Obtain the following:
1. Two apples, both of which must look good on the outside, but one of which must be bad on the inside. This can usually be told by looking for a small insect hole. If in doubt, cut the bad apple beforehand and push it together again.
2. A knife.
3. Two giant-size cardboard apples which can be opened up to show what they are like inside. Words are hidden on the insides and these can be pulled out when required (see diagram). The two halves of the apple are held together by paper clips or they can be hinged.

Introduction

Your singing was good! But how easy it is to sing sometimes without meaning the words. How easy it is to be a hypocrite. It's rather like some fruit, for example these two apples. (Produce the two real apples.) Both look good on the outside, but I wonder what they are like on the inside? (Make a show and suspense of cutting open the two apples.) If the heart of the apple is good, if the inside is good, then the whole apple will be good. In the same way it is important what we are like on the inside.

Story

Are you a hypocrite? No? Haven't you ever been quarrelling at home over some new birthday present, and then it's time to go to the Family Service? The moment you arrive back home, the old quarrel starts over again! It's not so much what we do, or look like, that matters, but rather what we are like on the inside. Let me show you what I mean.

Here are two giant apples:

1. This is good on the outside, but inside... (open) ugh! If we had left our bad apple much longer it would soon have been rotten all over. Paul in his letter to the Galatians gives a list of the rotten things that soon show in our lives if the Lord Jesus is not in control from the inside. Here are two of them:

   (a) Anger (Pull out of apple, and illustrate with an example of anger in the home.)

   (b) Pride (Pull out and illustrate.)

2. At first glance this apple is the same as the first. But the inside of this one is... (open) perfect! In the same chapter Paul goes on to list the good things which come from the person who trusts and obeys the Lord Jesus. Listen: 'The fruit of the Spirit is love, joy, peace, patience, kindness, goodness, faithfulness, gentleness, self-control.' What a contrast to the rotten fruit of 'anger' and 'pride'! Let's look at two of them more closely.

   (a) Love (pull out). If the Lord Jesus is in control of my life from the inside, then I will be more loving. Jesus once said, 'By this all men will know that you are my disciples, if you have love for one another' (John 13:35). Some people try by themselves to be right inside, and to love other people— in the family, at school, at work. Real love which cares for other people will not last unless it comes from a life controlled by Jesus.

   Just as an apple which is rotten inside can't stay good for very long, neither can the person who is not controlled from the inside by the Lord Jesus be really loving.

   (b) Joy (pull out). Contrast the temporary joy that people find in events or things, with the joy which comes from the certainty of God's purposes of love for us, as he is controlling us day by day, by his Holy Spirit.

Conclusion

The only way to be right on the outside is by admitting that on our own we cannot keep up good appearances; and then to go on and ask the Lord Jesus to come inside our lives, to control all we say and do and think. Then we will begin to see the love and joy and the rest of the characteristics that come instead of the anger and pride and other rotten marks. Which apple are you like?

Garry Guinness
Worthing

38   Harvest (4) Natural and Spiritual Growth

TEXTS

Matthew 7:15–20; Acts 9:1–2, 16:19–34; Galatians 5:22,23.

AIM

To show that the Christian life should result in a harvest which is just as natural as that which is expected from any tree or plant.

PREPARATION

Find or draw two large pictures of trees, each with three apples, oranges or pears on it. The fruit on the one tree is labelled 'hatred', 'quarrelling' and 'unhappiness', and on the

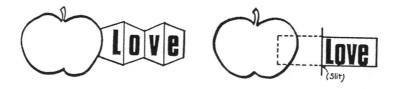

other 'joy', 'love', and 'peace'. The fruit can be hinged to the picture with sellotape at the top. A folded label can be concealed underneath, or a slit can be cut so that the label at the back of the picture can be pulled through.

Point of contact

Show fruit—orange, apple, pear (possibly picked out from harvest decoration in church). Talk about where and how each fruit grows. God gives the harvest. A tree without fruit is useless. Listen to what Jesus said about fruit trees: read Matthew 7:15–20.

1. *Jesus is really talking about people*

Have you ever thought that you are like a tree? (Show first picture.) There was a man once who was like this tree. Describe Saul as pictured in Acts 9:1,2. He hated the Christians (produce label 'hatred' from under one fruit). He wanted to destroy them—picked quarrels with them (produce label 'quarrelling'). Was he a happy man? He made himself and others unhappy. (Produce label 'unhappiness'.)

Refer to Jesus' words, 'A bad tree bears evil fruit.'

2. *Jesus is really talking about changed people*

(Show second picture.) Describe Paul as shown in Acts 16:19–34. Here is a man beaten because he is a Christian, and has just healed a girl in the name of Jesus—flung into a dark dungeon—feet in stocks. Yet he sings! (Produce label for 'joy'.) Earthquake—jailer about to commit suicide. Paul, 'Do yourself no harm' (produce label 'love'). A converted man and his family entertain the men who had previously been their enemies (produce label 'peace').

Conclusion

Saul/Paul—one and the same man. What made the difference? A Christian has God's life and power within him. He is different inside, so he bears different fruit. Some people try to alter the fruit they grow—'to be good'. But it is impossible without God's Spirit within them—just as impossible as expecting an orange to grow on an apple tree! Which tree is your life like?

Garth Grinham
Southport

39 Harvest (5) Decorations

Psalm 100:4. Reading: Luke 8:4–8.

Aim

Using the decorations in church to teach the need of thinking and thanking, sowing and growing.

Preparation

Be ready to refer to the fruit, flowers and vegetables which decorate the church (have examples to hand). See also that there is a packet of seeds within reach, and a tangle of brambles prominently displayed (refer to these in part B).

Arrange a display board as follows:

A Think and thank God's children
are like ours
B Seeds and weeds God's word
is like seed.
Your heart
is like soil.

A command: 'Give thanks to him' (Psalm 100:4).

A *Think and thank*

(Holding up examples for all to see.) Decoration, fruit and vegetables to make us think and so thank. No thanking without thinking.

God's children are like ours

Our children are not naturally thankful. You have to teach them (e.g. passing the butter, or coming from a party: 'What do you say?') Children take life for granted. They assume that they will have a home, clothes to wear, food to eat. They can't imagine life without them: but many do without in other parts of the world. But because our children's needs are met, they neither think nor thank. What is true of our children is also true of God's children. As God's children we must learn to thank. Too many grown-ups are like children all their lives: taking God's gifts for granted. Hence the commandment of Psalm 100:4: think and thank.

B *Seeds and weeds*

Ask if anyone can see any strange and unusual decorations in church (refer to the brambles).

1. Seeds

Notice two things. First, a seed has life inside it (eg a carrot, marrow or tomato seed—or even seeds of ancient Egypt, discovered and made to grow). Secondly, a seed must be in the right surroundings before it can grow at all. It won't grow in the packet. No growing without sowing.

God's word is like seed

Luke 8:11: 'The seed is the Word of God.' The same two things are true. First, there's life and power in God's word (cf 'Speak the word only...', Matthew 8:8. The valley of dry bones, Ezekiel 37:4,7). There's power in the word, and life too. Secondly, God's word must be in the right place. See Deuteronomy 6:6, 11:18; Psalm 119:11. The right place for God's word is in your heart. The Bible on the shelf is like seed in the packet. *God's word is like seed: your heart is like soil.* The seed's place is in the soil. No sowing: no growing.

2. *Weeds*

(Hold the tangle of brambles for all to see.) Your heart is like soil. There are two dangers. First: seeds and weeds (tell story of a girl or boy who stopped reading the Bible or stopped going to church because of other interests). The weeds choke the seed (Luke 8:7). Secondly: seeds or weeds. The danger of doing nothing. (Tell the story of a man who never touched his garden: it became a thicket of weeds.) Every year a harvest is certain: either of seeds or of weeds. So with your life and mine (cf parents who say, 'I don't believe in forcing him to go to church or Sunday school. Let him choose later on, when he is older'). Do nothing with a garden and what do you get? Nothing but weeds. What is true of nature is also true of human nature. It's seeds or weeds: no seeds, *all* weeds. The seed's place is in the soil (Deuteronomy 11:18−21).

Stephen Trapnell
Marlborough

40   Say it with Flowers!

TEXT

Matthew 6:28.

AIM

To declare the gospel message in the message of flowers. (This talk was originally given at a Family Harvest Service attended by an international Interflora Conference.)

PREPARATION

Make five very large cards, giant versions of the little card one receives with a gift of flowers.

1. Cover: I love you.   Inside: John 3:16a.
2. Cover: Get well soon.   Inside: Isaiah 1:18.
3. Cover: In loving memory.   Inside: Christ died for our sins and rose again.
4. Cover: Happy Birthday.   Inside: You must be born again—John 3:7.
5. Cover: Congratulations.   Inside: I give them eternal life—John 10:28.

PRESENTATION

Often we are not very good at knowing how to say something to someone, especially if it is a personal message, so to say it with flowers can help.

Jesus said we should consider God's message in the wild flowers that grow in the field. So what can God say to us in flowers today? Here are some typical message cards.

1. *I love you*

On Valentine's day, anniversaries etc. Flowers, like all the harvest, are a sign of God's loving care. Open the card and expand on John 3:16.

2. *Get well soon*

A very different message! Flowers are often sent to those in hospital. We might wish never to need those sorts of flowers. They tell us something is wrong. God's message is that we are in a sick and sinful world where much has gone wrong—and with us too! But flowers tell the sick to cheer up, for there is hope. God's promise to us in our sins gives us hope. Open up card and show Isaiah 1:18.

3. *In loving memory*

This is getting worse! But flowers are often used to pay our respects to the dead. God wants us to remember the death of Jesus and see on the cross the way he dealt with our sin. In his death and resurrection are forgiveness, hope and peace for us.

4. *Happy Birthday*

A mum received an enormous bunch of flowers from her transatlantic son last week. Flowers for a birthday. God wants us to have another birthday. Jesus said, 'You must be born again.' Recap cards 1, 2 and 3 and expound on the new birth at whatever length is appropriate.

5. *Congratulations*

Bouquets for a great success. Once we have begun the Christian life, we have an eternal future; we have eternal life.

Consider what the flowers say!

Ted Crofton
Cheltenham

41   Remembrance Sunday (1) The Poppy

TEXT

John 15:9–17.

AIM

To emphasise significant aspects of the Christian faith by using the letters P O P P Y.

PREPARATION

Using card make a large poppy with four petals and a centre, to build up during the talk. Each part has a letter or word on or beside it.

PRESENTATION

PRAISE for victory, peace, current international progress, for God's sovereignty, salvation.

OFFERING of those who gave their lives, bravery, suffering; of Jesus' life (Romans 5:8).

PRAYER for those who suffer because of war; for today's leaders; the Christian's secret weapon.

PEACE in the world, in all relationships (John 15:12), peace of God through Christ (John 3:16).

YOU. The personal application of the above.

Judith Rose
Rochester

42 Remembrance Sunday (2) From War to Peace

Text

Micah 4:1–4.

AIM

To change the letters of the word WAR to the word PEACE, during a sermon about changing a warlike world into a world of peace, perhaps by the process of beating swords into ploughshares.

PREPARATION

Prepare six letters on large cards: A; Y; R (so the bottom stroke can be covered up to represent P); V (without sharp point at the base of V so it can be turned through 90 degrees to represent C); E (so the bottom stroke can be covered up to represent F); and W (with each stroke of a similar length so that it can be inverted to represent the letter M, one stroke could be covered to represent the letter N and it can be turned through 90 degrees to represent the letter E). Also five volunteers.

PRESENTATION

Expound Scripture and current affairs as seems appropriate. At various intervals (to keep or regain attention) use a number of children holding up cards at the front. For a Parade Service, use representatives from each of the groups.

1. W A R

2. In Old Testament biblical times of war they needed an A R M Y (ask the child with W to invert it to make M. Ask another child to hold the letter Y. This can be done either by walking among the children and manhandling either them or the cards, or giving directions from the pulpit.)

3. In New Testament times the Romans had ships in a N A V Y (cover up one stroke of M to make N, remove R, and introduce V).

4. In wars today planes are used. In Britain we have our R A F (remove N, V and Y, bring back R and introduce F).

5. Our real hope, from the Bible, is for lasting P E A C E (cover the bottom stroke of R to make P, introduce E by uncovering the bottom stroke of F, introduce A, bring back the V through 90 degrees as C and reintroduce E from the M through 90 degrees).

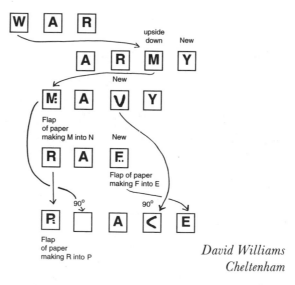

David Williams
Cheltenham

43   Remembrance Sunday (3) The Real War

TEXT

Ephesians 6:10–20.

AIM

To use Remembrance Sunday to alert people's attention to the spiritual war which still rages, but which has also already been won.

PREPARATION

Prepare a series of OHP acetates.

1. The heading *The real enemy* and the words 'the spiritual forces of evil in the heavenly realms'. Depict the devil as a snake, Jesus on the cross, a sword with blood on it, a gun and a bomb exploding.
2. One acetate with three parts, the first the whole sheet, the second and third able to be flipped over, because attached to the left edge of the main sheet. The artwork as follows:
   (a) The word *Powerful* and the text 'against the rulers... the authorities... the powers of this dark world'. Depict Jesus being tempted in the wilderness to accept 'all the kingdoms of the world'.
   (b) The word *Wicked* and the text 'spiritual forces of evil'.

Depict gas chamber and 6 million dead; 50 million died in two wars and the words 'Geneva Convention' crossed out.

(c) The word *Cunning* and the text 'the devil's schemes' with an angel but showing a snake's tail.

The following should each be in two parts.

3. (a) Depict Jesus from the cross shouting, 'It is finished' and a cross lying on top of a large dead snake.

(b) A Frenchman with beret and bow-tie holding a Union Jack on a pole and saluting.

4. (a) A font and the words from the baptism service either in full or in part: 'We should not be ashamed... to our lives' end.'

(b) A soldier in armour (a picture can be found in my book *More For All the Family* on page 174). Words 'truth', 'righteousness', 'peace'. Also an open Bible with a sword piercing through it so that the sharp end points towards the reader.

5. (a) A manger, person in armour brandishing a sword, trumpets.

(b) The famous World War One call-up picture, a bugle.

PRESENTATION

Ask what we are especially remembering today. Fill in briefly any important information omitted, such as the awfulness of war, the tremendous loss of life and the fact that some are still terribly disfigured. However, these two wars are illustrations of an even more important war that is still in progress. Ask for suggestions and refer to the above text that has already been read in the service, stressing verse 12.

Let's think together about the *real* conflict.

The real enemy (acetate 1)

Make reference to the devil in the Garden of Eden and to Jesus

in the wilderness and the evil people who plotted the crucifixion. Then give illustrations of evil, such as the story of David,
Bathsheba and Uriah the Hittite. (Children from an early age
know a lot about sex and probably need to grasp that its
misuse is sinful.) Refer to the latest horror stories in the media.
Then mention that none of us here is safe from this enemy: we
are too often not 'in love and charity with our neighbours'; we
may not actually murder or commit adultery, but we hate and
have impure thoughts (see Matthew 5:21–30). Perhaps
describe the Apostle Paul's inner conflict (Romans 7:21–23).

Mention a British general who once said that it is fatal to
underestimate your enemy and make a small war. We must
not do the same. Our enemy is *Powerful* (acetate 2a); refer to
Jesus in the wilderness; *Wicked* (acetate 2b)—mention that
our spiritual enemies used their powers destructively: 6 million died in gas chambers and 50 million in the two wars
together. They recognise no Geneva Convention. They hate
the light as we do when we give in to our temptations. Thirdly
these forces are *Cunning* (acetate 2c), so the devil likes either to
disguise himself as an angel of light or, better still, to deceive
people that he does not exist:

> The devil they fair voted out
> And of course the devil's gone.
> But simple folk would like to know
> Who carries his business on?

We can be encouraged, because all is not lost, Christianity
is good news. We can rejoice in:

The real victory

State that unlike the two world wars we remember today,
where the victory was by no means certain, the victory in the
real war was settled long ago by Jesus on the cross (show
acetate 3a and explain briefly the finished work of Christ).

Tell the story of the Frenchman who became a naturalised
Englishman. When asked what difference it had made he

explained that whereas previously he had lost the Battle of Waterloo now he had won it! (Acetate 3b.) Explain that when we accept Jesus as Saviour by repentance and faith, we transfer from being on the losing side of the devil to the winning side of Jesus.

The real war

Although victory has been achieved, the war is not over. Evil spiritual forces are all around us encouraging us to defect and become traitors to the Christian cause. Refer to the need to take the statement made at our baptism very seriously (show acetate 4a). But how? Comment on the Christian armour mentioned in text, as time allows (show acetate 4b). Only as we put on the whole spiritual armour will we be able to stand (verse 13).

The real Armistice

Paul begins our text with 'Finally', which has the meaning of 'henceforth' or 'for the remaining time'. He wants us to understand that from the first coming of Jesus at the first Christmas to his final coming at the end of the world we have to be fighting in the spiritual war (acetate 5a). If we are not aware of this conflict it can only mean that we are on the wrong side, because the devil does not bother those who are still his own. We need to repent of our sins and believe in Jesus.

But for those who know the truth then let today be a day to rouse ourselves to the spiritual fight (acetate 5b). There will be no cessation of hostilities, no temporary truce or cease-fire until the end of life or history, when the real Armistice is declared and eternal peace is ushered in.

Perhaps quote Revelation 3:21 and 21:4.

Has everyone here today joined up in the *real* war?

Michael Botting
Editor

44   An Anniversary Talk—In Jesus

Text

2 Corinthians 5:17.

Aim and method

To summarise the Christian faith by means of an elaborate visual aid that will be appreciated by all ages. It is based on an original idea of the late Dr Ernest Kevan, one time principal of London Bible College. The work and cost involved may seem a bit daunting, but it is the sort of talk you could well take with you to another church where you have been asked to speak on a special occasion, though it may well be wise to check that the congregation has not heard and seen it already!

Preparation

Construct eight boxes of various sizes so that each fits into the other. It is only necessary to have four of the six sides of each box, as the back and the base are not visible to the congregation. The boxes can be quite easily constructed out of hardboard and stuck together with Bostick. The boxes should have on them in the following order, going from the largest to the smallest, 'Jesus', 'Sin' with a cross stuck across it, 'Power', 'Bible', 'Prayer', 'Church', 'Joy', 'Heaven'. The size of the boxes should be such that when placed on a table and built up with the smallest box at the top, the speaker is unable to put

the last box up without standing on a chair or stool to do so. Convenient dimensions of the largest box could be—front face, height 12″, width 13″; depth of box 9¼″. The next box— front face 11½″, width 12½″; depth 9″, and the proportions of each box decreasing by the same amount each time. At the beginning of the talk the boxes should be packed one inside the other and covered with a black cloth.

PRESENTATION

Refer to the fascination our grandparents or great grand-parents seemed to have about cemeteries. Mention the statement on many tombstones of the words 'In Christ' or 'In Jesus'. Hence refer to the text. What does it mean to be 'In Jesus'? Reveal the boxes with the front box showing the word 'Jesus'. Remove the box and place alongside of the others to reveal 'Sin' crossed out and enlarge on how Christ's death on the cross made it possible for God to forgive (cancel) our sins. Hence reveal each of the boxes, gradually building them higher and higher as you talk on each subject. Before going on to the next box, recap by saying that to be 'in Jesus' means sin forgiven, the power of the Holy Spirit, the Bible coming alive, prayer becoming real, the church becoming a fellowship and an inward joy even in the midst of trouble. When you reach the final box, but before you show it, state that there is something different about this box from all the others. Whereas they refer to Christian experience in this life, the last refers to the Christian life after physical death. Hence reveal 'Heaven' and step up on the chair or stool to put the box on top. Speak briefly about heaven and ask the congregation whether they can say they know the truth of these things because they are 'in Jesus'. You can either end the talk by packing all the boxes away and recapping as you do so or deliberately leave the boxes piled up as a reminder to the congregation before they leave the church.

Michael Botting
Editor

The Christian Life

45 What Is Sin?

TEXT

1 John 5:16–20. (See also Romans 3:23; Ephesians 2:1; Hebrews 2:2–3; 1 John 3:4; Romans 1:18.)

AIM

To explain some of the different words for sin in the New Testament; and to show that rebellion against God is the sin that leads to spiritual death.

PREPARATION

Either obtain from a toy or novelty shop the Cling Ball game that involves throwing ping-pong balls that stick to the target by means of Velcro; or make such a game as follows:

Obtain a piece of light-coloured (eg yellow) brushed nylon,

The numbers on the target are of no special significance.

roughly 35cm x 45cm and draw on it, using indelible paint or marker-pen, three concentric circles of radii 4cm, 10cm, and 16cm. Then divide the circles as shown on the diagram above.

To complete the game obtain at least three (but no more than five) table-tennis balls and attach to each two strips of (hook) Velcro to go round the middle at right-angles to each other: the strips should be 7mm wide.

In addition prepare five instruction cards to be given to five volunteers from the congregation. (If possible choose the 'volunteers' beforehand, and make sure they understand exactly what they have to do!) The cards should have the following words on them:

1. Aim, but throw wide so as to miss the target completely.
2. Go for a really big throw, but then fall over before you can let go of the ball.
3. Aim, then take a big step forward to make it easier to hit the target.
4. Aim, but when my back is turned, run up so close that you are able to place the ball in the centre of the target.
5. Say 'No!' when I ask you to have a go. When I insist, say: 'Don't tell *me* what to do. I'm not playing your silly game!'

Also prepare five cards with the following Bible verses on them:

1. Romans 3:23
2. Ephesians 2:1
3. Hebrews 2:2–3
4. 1 John 3:4
5. Romans 1:18

These cards should be given to five different volunteers before the service.

PRESENTATION

Hang the target in such a place that all the congregation can see it and the children can attempt to hit it. Mark a 'throwing line' on the floor or use a convenient carpet edge or piece of furniture.

Begin, if you like, by telling the (very old) story of the time when a vicar was leaving a parish and various people were expressing their gratitude to him. One person said: 'You have been so helpful to us all, Vicar; we never knew what sin was until you came to this parish!'

Then explain that you have asked five volunteers to help you demonstrate just what the Bible means when it talks about sin.

1. *The first child throws and misses.* Explain that one of the Bible words for sin is *hamartia*, which means failure, or missing the mark. Point out that this word occurs in Romans 3:23, and ask your first reader to read that verse. Elaborate with reference to Romans 7:19—'For what I do is not the good I want to do; no the evil I do not want to do—this I keep on doing.'

   Mention Jesus' rebuke to Peter after his confession that Jesus is the Christ.

2. *The second child goes to throw but falls over. Paraptoma* means transgression, or slipping up. The word occurs in Ephesians 2:1. Second reader reads that verse. Elaborate with reference to 1 Corinthians 10:12—'So if you think you are standing firm, be careful that you don't fall!' Mention Peter denying Jesus.

3. *The third child takes a big step forward and throws. Parabasis* means iniquity or stepping over the line. The word occurs in Hebrews 2:2. Third reader reads that verse. Elaborate

with reference to 1 Timothy 6:10—'Some people, eager for money have wandered from the faith and pierced themselves with many griefs.' Mention Judas Iscariot and his betrayal of Jesus.

4. *Call fourth child to have a go and make a point of not looking to see what he does. Perhaps start picking up the balls already thrown.* Anomia means lawlessness. The word occurs in 1 John 3:4. Fourth reader reads that verse. Elaborate with reference to Galatians 5:13—'You were called to be free men; only do not turn your freedom into licence for your lower nature.' Refer to Jesus' condemnation of the Pharisees.

5. *Ask fifth child to throw and express surprise at the refusal. Adikia* means rebellion or unrighteousness. The word occurs in Romans 1:18. Fifth reader reads that verse. Elaborate with reference to Romans 2:8—'For those who are governed by selfish ambition, who refuse obedience to the truth, and take wrong for their guide, there will be the fury of retribution.' Mention the parable of the unfaithful and disobedient servant.

Conclusion

Recap the various stages of sin, reminding everyone that though we all sin, in Christ there is forgiveness for all, provided that we are honest and humble enough to ask for God's forgiveness. But if we spurn God's love in Christ and refuse to listen to the truth about ourselves (refusing to 'play the game') then we shall end up cut off from God for all eternity.

David McIntosh
Ellesmere Port

46   Washing Powders

TEXT

Isaiah 1:16–20 or Revelation 1:1–7.

PREPARATION

Obtain the following packets of washing powders and soft-
eners from a shop or supermarket: Fairy Snow, Lux, Dreft,
Surf, Bounce, Bold, and Comfort.

Draw pictures of the containers on acetates for overhead
projection, but change the names:

> Fairy Snow becomes Fairly Slow
> Lux   becomes Lax
> Dreft   becomes Drift
> Surf   becomes Self

Bounce, Bold and Comfort stay the same. You will produce
each container as the talk proceeds and pretend its name is the
one on the acetate.

PRESENTATION

Begin by explaining that when you came back from holiday
you had lots of dirty washing and that you went to the supermarket and wondered which powder to use. The powders
reminded you of the people in the pews. What sort of Christian

are we? Some powders are better at washing than others, and some people behave better as Christians than others. Go through the poor ones: Fairly Slow—those who do not grow very fast in the Christian life; Lax—the lazy; Drift—those who go along with the crowd; and Self—those who are selfish. Contrast these with the good powders and conditioners like Bounce—the joyful Christian; Comfort—those who put an arm round you and care; Bold—like Peter and John on the day of Pentecost, for example.

You can also use other pictures to illustrate the points you wish to make. For example, for Fairly Slow, show a sunflower with a long, tall stem looking down at a shrunken weed. Explain that the sunflower grows fast because it is close to the sun, but the weed is starved of good food—like a Christian who does not feed on God's word.

There is a cleaner recently produced called Frend. You can, if you wish, add this to the list and end your talk by explaining that the Lord is our Friend, who helps us to overcome our faults and to be better Christians.

Christopher Porteous
Beckenham

47 Faith

TEXTS

Mark 5:24–34; Ephesians 2:8.

AIM

To show that faith is not merely belief in a certain thing, but an attitude which results in a response to Jesus.

PREPARATION

Large, simple flannelgraph pictures, including one of an out-stretched hand, would be a useful visual aid.

PRESENTATION

Point of contact

Have you ever been ill? For how long? Who, or what, made you better? Can you imagine being ill for a year? For five years? Even for *twelve* years? Turn to miracle in Mark 5:24–34.

1. *Woman and her plight.* Verses 25 and 26. She desperately needed help, but there was no one who could help her.

2. *No one to help?* Verse 27. She had heard of Jesus. She believed that Jesus could help her. Was it enough to 'believe' it?

3. *What could she do?* Verses 27–29. Jesus was passing through—Jairus—crowd. Woman dared not interrupt, or call out. Stretched out and touched his cloak. (Ceremonial uncleanness forbade even to touch! Yet she did.) Immediately felt well.

4. *Jesus knew.* Verse 30. Jesus always knows when anyone turns towards him, even though nobody else sees. The disciples (and in particular Peter, who was probably nearest to Jesus) were sceptical (verse 31) but Jesus knew.

5. *The woman confesses.* Verse 33. And Jesus says rather a strange thing (verse 34).

6. *What did Jesus mean by faith?* Show picture of outstretched hand. Talk about why we stretch out a hand (e.g. to grasp hold, to give, to shake or hold hands). Indicates relationship between people. Faith is like stretching out our hand to Jesus because, like this woman, we need help—and no one can help us like Jesus. Note verse 34: *'your faith'* has made you well—not in fact the touch. When we stretch out our hand, Jesus himself clasps it and keeps firm hold of it.

Conclusion

Refer to Ephesians 2:8, 'not your own doing'. Give example of climber stranded on cliff. Cannot haul himself up, *can* stretch out his hand to the one who is reaching out to save him.

Garth Grinham
Southport

48   Conversion

TEXT

Luke 19:1–10.

AIM

To encourage people to search diligently for Christ.

PREPARATION

There are three possible visual aids. The simplest is to use four children to hold up four words in turn. A picture such as flannelgraph could be used to build up the story, or an overhead projector used to picture the incidents. But the words need to be shown somehow.

PRESENTATION

Introduction

Describe Zacchaeus the man and the kind of work he did. A civil servant working for the Romans and greatly disliked by all. Note he was also deceitful and possibly a thief. Be sure to point out that everything was 'above board' and he was very ordinary, just like most of us. Now go through the following four stages in developing the story. He made (show the words):

1. *A great* DISCOVERY: In spite of his wealth, nice home, etc, life was very empty and he was not happy. Peace and happiness cannot be bought. He had:

2. *A great* DESIRE: This was to be different. To be happy like some other people he knew. To be liked and to be a much better person. He was so dissatisfied with life as it was— there must be something better somewhere. He evidently heard about Jesus and began to seek him (verse 3), not realising Jesus was also seeking him (verse 10). This aroused in him:

3. *A great* DETERMINATION: That was to see Jesus for himself. He would go to any lengths to see for himself and not just listen to what others had to say. Tell of his experiences in the tree and his conversation with Jesus. Stress the invitation Jesus gave him (verse 5). Note the word 'must' (RSV). Finally he made:

4. *A great* DECISION: It was really twofold, one leading on to the other.
He invited Jesus into his home.
He invited Jesus into his heart.

Conclusion

Notice what Jesus had to say about it (verse 9). Show what a difference this made. Zacchaeus was a changed man (verse 8). This is the real reason why Jesus came. Encourage the congregation to make the same decision as Zacchaeus.

Donald Churchman
Hayling Island

49 Hands

TEXT

Luke 24:36–40.

AIM

To show the worthwhileness of committing one's life into the hands of Christ.

PREPARATION

Everybody has brought their own visual aid with them. This is useful as a talk which has to be given at very short notice or when it is difficult to use a normal type visual aid. Ask everyone to look at their own hands. At each point they could look at their hands again.

PRESENTATION

Introduction

Why should Jesus want to show his hands to the disciples? We can tell quite a lot about people if we look at their hands. Their individuality—finger prints. Their character perhaps—the way they shake hands. Their job—the miner, for instance, compared with an office clerk. Their health—a doctor will often ask to look at a patient's hands, especially nails (do you bite yours?). Whether a person is married or engaged perhaps. What did they discover when they saw the hands of Jesus?

1. Salvation

This is a long word and needs explaining. There is the well-known story of the mother who saved her baby from a fire and received severe burns on her hands as a result. She usually wore gloves. One day the little girl, now at school, saw her mother's scarred hands and said how horrible they were. Her father told her the story when he came home from work that night, and she immediately went to her mother and asked whether she could see again those beautiful hands. So with the scars of Jesus, but he saved us from sin, not flames (Isaiah 49:16).

2. Strength

Retell the story of the time Jesus reached out with his hand to save Peter from the rough sea. He is able to keep us through every storm in life. No one can take us from him, there is complete safety in his hands. He will keep us (John 10:27–29).

3. Skill

This may seem a little obscure but it is an important part of our Lord's dealing with us, and we may be helped to see how worthwhile his friendship and leading are (see Psalm 78:72). Notice also: being tempted in all points, etc. He is also able to help us. Like a father helping a child along a difficult and unknown path. The incident of Jesus controlling an unbroken colt could be used to good effect here.

Conclusion

Invite those present to put their lives into the hands of Christ.

Donald Churchman
Hayling Island

50 Obedience

Luke 5:1–11.

To show, from Peter's encounter with Jesus, what it means to obey the Lord.

Point of contact

Produce live animal(s); show how we have to train an animal to be obedient, for its own happiness and safety. Talk of ways in which *we* are asked to be obedient—for our own happiness and safety. Eg in the home, at school, on roads, at seaside.

1. Jesus gave Peter a command (verse 4)

   (a) It was not a very *convenient* thing for Simon Peter to have to do. He was already very tired. He had washed his nets, ready for next night's fishing.

   Compare (in mime form): missionary family all prepared to go to one field (India). Baggage packed, language learned. Suddenly door closed—only to be called by God to go to Africa! New language, culture,

215

climate. Was it *convenient* to be asked to make such a big change?

(b) It did not seem a very *sensible* thing to ask. Morning was a bad time for fishing (it may even have been noon by this time). Anyway, Jesus was a carpenter—what did he know about where and when to fish?

Compare (in mime form): Miss Gladys Aylward— poor, ill-educated, turned down by missionary society. Was it *sensible* to go to China in the way she did?

(c) It was not an *easy* command to obey. In one sense, fishing was the easiest thing in the world for Peter to do, but in these circumstances he would have to sink his pride and face the possibility of being made to look a fool in front of the crowds possibly still thronging the shore.

Compare (in mime form): Bishop David Sheppard. Was it *easy* for him to give up outstanding career in first-class cricket for 'full-time' Christian service?

2. *In spite of all these things*, Peter obeyed Jesus' word (verse 5).

Elaborate on the importance of obeying what we hear from God's word (James 1:22). 'If he is not Lord of all, he is not Lord at all.' Every aspect of our lives to be under his command.

3. *Result of Peter's obedience* (verses 6 and 7)

Just what he most needed and most wanted, but couldn't get by his own efforts—happiness and satisfaction.

Conclusion

Introduce examples of ways in which we are asked to be obedient to God, eg loving, trusting, patient, strong—they may not be *convenient*, *easy* or *sensible*, but will lead to same result.

Garth Grinham
Southport

51   Be Shaped but Don't Be Squeezed!

TEXT

Romans 12:2 (J.B. Phillips version).

AIM

To show the importance of allowing God to shape our lives in his way rather than letting the world around us squeeze us into its mould.

PREPARATION

This is an object talk. You will need to obtain: two articles of pottery that have been made by a potter—one made on a potter's wheel, eg, a jug or vase; and the second made by shaping the clay, eg, a figure, animal or shape. You will also need an orange and an orange/lemon squeezer, and a jelly and a jelly mould.

PRESENTATION

1. Tell congregation the title of the talk and inform them that you will use it throughout as a refrain.
    Minister: 'Be shaped'
    Congregation: 'But don't be squeezed.'
    This becomes both humorous and a good aid to memory to

illustrate the talk. Use the refrain a number of times throughout the talk, and also later in the worship itself.

2. *Shaped by God*
   (a) Explain how the potter had to shape your pottery visual aids—show congregation.
   (b) Mention how God is compared to a potter in Jeremiah chapter 18.
   (c) Relate how God shapes our lives today.
      —By the teaching of Jesus in the Bible and in the church.
      —By the presence of the Holy Spirit in our lives, experienced in our joyful and victorious living, and in our worship and prayers.
   (d) Mention how Paul's letter to the Romans (his Good News) is in two parts—*Belief* and *Behaviour*. The two go together when we allow God to shape our lives.

3. *Squeezed by the world*
   (a) Take the orange, cut it in half and get one of the children to squeeze out the juice into the orange/lemon squeezer, then into a cup.
   (b) Take the jelly and explain how it is made into liquid and then poured into the jelly mould to come out set in that shape. (You could even arrange to do it.)
   (c) Explain how we can be squeezed into the world's way unless God is in control of our lives, just like the orange was squeezed. Describe how, without God, we are just like jelly and we let the world constrict us just as it wants into its own mould. Use the following examples to explain how this happens:
      —school behaviour
      —work practice
      —neighbours' attitudes
      Too easily our attitude can become: number one first, a rat race, one-upmanship.

4. Read Romans 12:2 (J.B. Phillips). The lesson we learn from all that is to let God shape our lives so that we may live to his glory.

Ray Adams
Redditch

22.6.03

52 What Does Baptism Mean?

TEXT

Acts 16:16–34.

AIM

To explain the meaning of baptism, perhaps because a baptism is taking place in the Family Service.

PREPARATION

Have the words 'Forgiveness', 'Faith', 'Fight', 'Family' and 'Fun' ready to be revealed at the appropriate moment as you tell the story of the Philippian jailer. The words could be made of fluorescent paper stuck on to five pieces of rectangular black card, different coloured paper being used for each word.

PRESENTATION

There are several references in the New Testament to family baptisms. For example, Cornelius, the Roman soldier, was converted to Jesus Christ and he and all his family were baptised.

What is baptism? It is a visible sign of something that is difficult to put into words. We use signs for lots of things. A kiss is a sign of love, a salute is a sign of loyalty, and a handshake of friendship. At a wedding the bride is given a ring to wear to show she is married.

What does baptism mean? It means all that is really meant by being a Christian. Let us look at another story in Acts where a baptism takes place. Briefly tell the story of the Philippian jailer. Put up the word cards making the following points:

1. *Forgiveness*

   The jailer was a sinner. He needed salvation, including the forgiveness of his sins (verse 31). The reason why water is used in baptism is because it illustrates the washing away of sin.

2. *Faith*

   The jailer had to have faith in the Lord Jesus (verse 31), the One who had died for his sins on the cross.

3. *Fight*

   The Christian life is not easy. It is a fight. Paul and Silas were beaten and thrown into prison because of their witness to Jesus (verses 22–24).

4. *Family*

   But to be a Christian means that you are welcomed into a new family. Reference could be made to the church that had begun in the house of Lydia.

5. *Fun*

   Finally, the Christian life is also fun. For all their trials and troubles the apostles and the jailer and his household rejoiced (verses 25, 33 and 34).

If a baptism is actually to take place, appropriate parts of the service can be quoted to illustrate the above points, eg on 'Fight'—'manfully to fight under his banner'.

Michael Botting
Editor

53 The Church—Members One of Another

TEXT

1 Corinthians 12.

AIM

To show how we all need one another (personal responsibility).

PREPARATION

A bag of golf clubs can be used with good effect.

PRESENTATION

1. In the church of Jesus Christ we all have different gifts (verse 11). Apart from those listed in Chapter 12 there are the practical gifts such as flower-arranging, teaching, carpentry, writing, typing, gardening, etc (verses 4–7). Just as golf clubs are all different and made for different jobs (explain this by showing the various types and angles of the irons) so are we all.

2. The trouble is, when work needs to be done so often the right people are not there to do it (verses 17–19). Just imagine how a golfer would feel on the first tee if he had left

his driver at home, or if he went in a bunker and hadn't got his sand-iron, or arrived on the first green only to discover his putter was still in the club house. See also 1 Timothy 4:14 and 2 Timothy 1:6.

3. One thing God does expect from all his helpers is that they are thoroughly prepared for the work he has for them to do. You cannot do God's work if you are not clean and ready, any more than you can use a golf club if it has lumps of dirt on it (2 Timothy 2:21). Stress the need for spiritual as well as practical efficiency. We need to be our very best for God.

4. Any golfer will tell you that the golf club needs to be held firmly in the hand. Each day we also need to commit our lives into the hands of Christ (John 10:27–29).

Donald Churchman
Hayling Island

54 The Church—Foundations, Cornerstone and Building

TEXTS

Acts 2:42, 47 and 1 Peter 2:4–8.

AIM

To explain (a) the foundations, (b) the cornerstone and (c) the building of God's church.

PREPARATION

Prepare four long cards, with the words 'Apostles' teaching' and 'Breaking of Bread' on two strips of card approx 30″ x 5″, and the words 'Fellowship' and 'Prayers' on two shorter strips of card approx 20″ x 5″. Obtain, or make, a cubic box (approx 10″ sides), with the letters C H R I S T, one on each face. Collect, over a period of time, 20–30 or more shoe boxes that can be built up as walls, suitably painted for colour coding on each layer of the building, with names or qualities written on them as determined by the points made in section 3. These are given out to the congregation in advance. Also a big table is needed at the front to build this church.

Introduction

Jesus once told story about two men, one wise and one foolish...now when Jesus built his church, we can expect him to be very wise. What's the first thing needed?

1. *Foundations.* The Bible tells us what these are (Acts 2:42). Talk about each one in turn and lay flat on the table as in the diagram below. (Theologically you may wish to point out from 1 Corinthians 3:11 that the basic foundation is Christ himself, on which comes this next layer of foundations.)

2. *The Cornerstone.* The next question is how to get all the walls straight, and the corners right. In the old days they didn't have our modern instruments. They went to a builder's yard to look for a cornerstone—literally, for the corner of the house—and then built along from that. So let's imagine you've gone to a builder's yard. He's got nothing that seems right. You ask to go round the back—'Oh, there's nothing there, it's my scrap yard,' he says. You go and look, and almost stumble over a half-hidden stone: you unearth it—and it's perfect: every angle exactly 90 degrees. 'I'll have this stone that the other builders rejected.' Show cube, the letters of C H R I S T on each face. (See also Psalm 118:22–23; Matthew 21:42; Ephesians 2:20.)

   You put your cornerstone in place. You get close to it and eye along one direction, which is where you are going to build one wall, then the other wall, and then upwards. You must go back every time to the cornerstone, to ensure you are building straight, and that you are true to the original.

3. Let's go on then and build with bricks. Today, plenty of you have got shoe boxes, which we'll be using. Ask for these in groups, as explained later. Now as we build, it has to be on these original foundations (back to the Bible) and true to

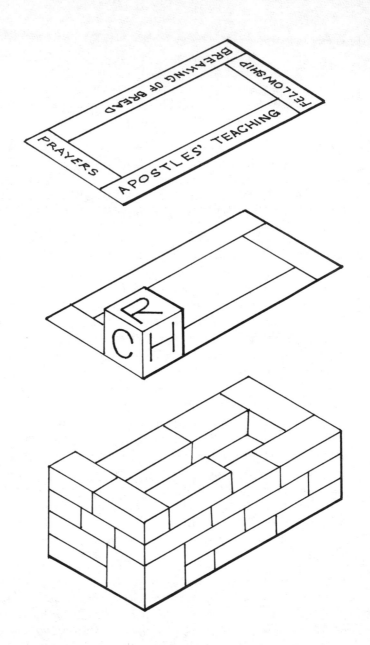

the cornerstone—keep looking along to check. Look to the Scriptures; look back through the years of history to the early church; look to the apostolic foundation; look at the bricks either side of you, to see what the master builder is doing in other churches. (See also 1 Peter 2:4.)

4. So we build, or rather let him build his church (Matthew 16:18), indwelt by the Holy Spirit (1 Corinthians 3:16).

5. Remember, we have been building the church. We can keep adding boxes, or people. Indeed we must keep building. The church only grew by evangelism, as the Lord added to them (Acts 2:47).

Notes

(a) With lots of people bringing boxes it shows the importance of each and every person.

(b) The boxes could be labelled with people's names (eg, Apostles themselves—they go on the first layer, then people like Stephen, Timothy etc, and eventually modern names, making it easier for people to bring the boxes in the right order.

(c) The boxes could alternatively be labelled (colour coded) with qualities that God looks for in his church: eg Light, Salt, Fruit, Gifts, Love, Service, Outreach, etc.

David Williams
Cheltenham

55 Prayer

Texts

Nehemiah 2:4; Matthew 6:6; Mark 1:35; Luke 6:12.

Aim

To encourage the development of prayer as an essential part of the Christian life.

Preparation

A simple large model telephone with moveable dial and ear and mouthpiece can be an effective visual aid.

Presentation

Point of contact

Talk about it being the most natural thing for friends to talk to one another, for a child to talk to and confide in his father.

1. *Prayer is a conversation between ourselves and God*

   Jesus himself gives examples of this (Luke 6:12; Mark 1:35; John 17). Illustration of telephone conversation. When we phone somebody:
   (a) We must make up our minds to dial their number—determine to contact them.

(b) We must concentrate and shut out other voices (reason for phone boxes), see Matthew 6:6. Quote:

> I often say my prayers, but do I ever pray?
> And do the wishes of my heart go with the words I say?
> I may as well kneel down and worship gods of stone
> As offer to the living God a prayer of words alone.

(c) We must listen for the other person to speak.

(d) We cannot see one another, but we know that the contact is real—we recognise voice of friend or loved one.

(e) There can be interference on the line which spoils the conversation.

(f) We *can* slam the receiver down! Do we do this with God? *But* unlike our earthly phone conversations, God's number is never engaged!

2. *Prayer can be an SOS in an emergency*

Eg, Nehemiah. Illustration of a 'walkie-talkie' radio used by police, soldiers, etc.

3. *Prayer is a means of guidance and instruction*

Eg, Paul's experiences, especially on missionary journeys. Illustration of astronauts in touch with mission control, instructed to make contact with HQ at regular intervals.

Conclusion

Sing (solo or congregation) 'Prayer is the soul's sincere desire' or 'I often say my prayers'.

Garth Grinham
Southport

56 The Underground of Life

John 1:12.

AIM

To show the difference between the man who is unconverted and the man who is a Christian, and a victorious Christian.

PREPARATION

Obtain a large map of the London Underground from the publicity department of London Transport. Pin the map to a board, and write on pieces of card the names of your two underground lines, 'Circle Line' and 'Victorious Line'. Cut out of cardboard four station names in the form seen on the underground, ie, a circle with a bar across it. On one side write the Circle Line station names: Hatch End, Snaresbrook, Broadway and Mile End; on the other side the Victorious Line stations: King's Cross, Temple, Narrow (altered from Harrow) and White City (this could also be Mansion House). Put on the map four hooks to hang the stations on, and one for the name of the line.

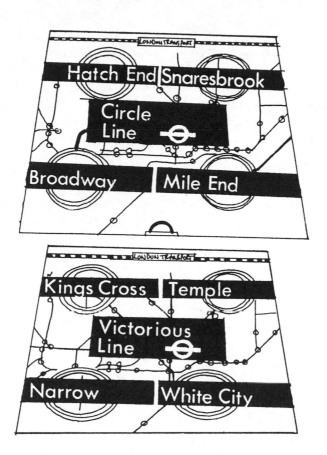

PRESENTATION

Begin by telling the congregation that you are going to take them for a ride on the underground, and put up your map. This underground is called the underground of life, and is a picture of what life is like. Then put up on the board the words 'Circle Line' and explain that this is the line that many people are living on without God. It is called the Circle Line because you get nowhere on it except round in circles. 'Hatch End' is birth, 'Snaresbrook' is temptation, 'Broadway' is the way that leads to destruction, and 'Mile End' is death. Give each station to a child who brings it forward and hangs it on a hook as you ask for it, until all four stations are up. Then explain that those who want to live for God travel on a different line, the 'Victorious Line' (put up those words on the map). Turn over the stations already put up on the board to reveal the names of the new stations. You change at 'King's Cross' because it is through Christ's death that we can claim victory. You go on to 'Temple' because the true and victorious Christian seeks to worship with God's people in church, then to 'Narrow', because the narrow way leads to eternal life. Finally the Christian comes to 'White City', which is heaven.

Conclude by asking which line they are travelling on, and suggest that the Victorious Line should be on their ticket now.

Christopher Porteous
Beckenham

57   Christian Witness

Matthew 5:14–16.

Aim

To show that Christians should be lights in the world.

Preparation

The following equipment will be needed:

200 (or 150) watt bulb
100 watt bulb
two-way switch
two bayonet sockets, one switched
approx 12′ of twinflex
two-pin plug

Separate the two strands of flex and connect as in the diagram. Stick a small piece of celluloid (or similar substance) about the size of a penny to the shiny terminals at the base of the brighter bulb. This will stop the flow of current.

The aim of the wiring in series is to produce a dimming effect so that the current can be divided between the two bulbs. Mark both switches so that you know which position is 'on'. Either arrange the circuit so that the 100 watt bulb is

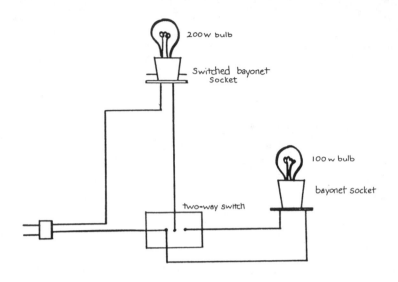

hidden, or have a box to put over it (in this case less flex will be needed).

Discuss the way that lights stand out in darkness. Illustrate by a local example (eg, the light on the Post Office tower).

In Matthew 5:14 Jesus was speaking to his disciples. He meant them to stand out from others and be noticed. And so must we as Christians today. Jesus did not say, 'You must be the light in the world.' He said, 'You *are* the light of the world!'

What's the good of a faith that makes no difference; that can't be seen? The test of anything today is: does it work? Does it make a difference? People will only turn to Christ in so far as they see that he makes a difference in our lives. It is Christ's purpose that each of us who belong to him should shine for him.

Illustrate with the 200 watt bulb, the brightest that can easily be bought.

1. Its purpose is to shine. If it no longer works, it is called a dud, and thrown away. It is only useful as long as it shines. So with the Christian.

2. It can't shine by itself. It depends on power from outside itself in order to shine. So too with the Christian.

   It is sadly true that while Jesus says to his followers, 'You are the light of the world,' the vast majority of them live very ordinary lives, which are not in any way distinctive, except when it is time to go to church. The rest of the week they live like others who have no faith in Christ.

3. Why is it that Christians so often do not shine?

   (a) *Something missing*. Place the 200 watt bulb in its socket. Show surprise that it does not light. Follow the lead back and find that it is not plugged in. No contact! Of course it will not shine! Have you made contact with Jesus Christ?

   (b) *Something between*. Plug in and try all the switches. Still it does not light. (Again, show surprise!) Remove the 200 watt bulb and examine it, discovering the celluloid circle glued to the base. Of course it does not work, there is something in between! It stops the power. Sin is like that: something which can be so small, but effectively stops us from shining for Christ. 'Something in between' which must be removed. (Remove the celluloid disc, and illustrate by explaining cataract operation on the eye.)

   (c) *Something else*. Plug in the light bulb and switch on. With the two-way switch previously positioned at 'on', the 200 watt bulb will barely glow (while the hidden 100 watt bulb will shine brightly). Joke about the brightest bulb barely shining at all! Explain how this is achieved: that the greater part of the power goes to the concealed smaller bulb. Show how this is true so often in our lives, as other interests cause us to be half-

235

hearted Christians and Jesus has possession of only half of our heart. Divided loyalties can easily mean that we are not shining as brightly as we should. Jesus had harsh things to say about lukewarm Christians! Half-heartedness means that only part of Christ's power is to be seen in our lives.

(d) *Something startling!* Switch the two-way switch and watch people blink! (The 100 watt is isolated, and the power now goes to the 200 watt bulb which shines brightly.) Full power means full light. 'You are the light of the world.' Jesus means his followers today to shine like this so that those about us blink with surprise. 'Let your light so shine...' (Matthew 5:16).

Stephen Trapnell
Marlborough

58   Hope

TEXTS

Romans 4:18–21, 15:13; Hebrews 6:11–20; 1 Timothy 1:1;
1 John 3:2, 3.

AIM

To show what hope means to the Christian.

PREPARATION

Obtain pictures of boy and girl cut from magazines, and draw
a simple outline of a ship at anchor. You will also need three
cards with the words: 'Hope keeps me happy'; 'Hope keeps me
strong'; 'Hope keeps me trusting'.

PRESENTATION

Point of contact

Show pictures of boy and girl. Introduce them as John and
Jill. John is a good athlete. He is *hoping* to break the school
record for 100 metres. Jill is good at acting. She is *hoping* to be
the main part in the school play.

1. John—no chocolate cake for tea—he must keep his weight
   down.

Jill—no television-viewing—must spend time memorising words for school play.

They don't grumble or moan—they *hope* for something better.

Produce card: Hope keeps me happy (Romans 15:13, J. B. Phillips).

2. John—gets up early and spends much free time in training.

Jill—spends much of her spare time rehearsing.

They have one thing in mind—they keep on—they do not give up—because of their *hope*.

Produce card: Hope keeps me strong (Hebrews 6:11, 12).

3. Abraham—story of man who 'hoped against hope' (Romans 4:18–21). He trusted God's promises—*hoped*.

John—believes his coach when he tells him he has a chance of breaking the record.

Jill—trusts her teacher's word that she is good enough for the part.

Produce card: Hope keeps me trusting.

This is *why* I can be happy, and persevere.

Conclusion

Show simple outline of ship at anchor (Hebrews 6:19, 20). A ship (my life) will often meet storms, or be near dangerous rocks. Sailor throws out anchor ('hope') which can embed deeply (in God's love), and the ship is held firm and safe.

What are we hoping for? Give suggestions of other 'temporary' hopes like John and Jill's (eg, better exam results, better home, better job). What is the Christian's hope? (Eager expectation.) What is the ground of a Christian's hope? See 1 Timothy 1:1: 'Jesus...our hope.' He saves us, keeps us; one day we shall see him and be like him (1 John 3:2, 3).

Garth Grinham
Southport

59 Life's So Unfair

Texts

Matthew 20:1–16 main Lesson, which could be read dramatically. Philippians 4:11–13 and 1 Peter 2:22–24 to be read during the talk by forewarned readers, when called upon by the preacher.

Aim

To teach from Jesus' controversial parable that none of us can demand rights from God, but his grace is our salvation.

Preparation

Prepare a series of OHP acetates as follows:

1. The words 'It's not fair...!' Under it a rough sketch of the outside of a modern facade of a job centre.
2. Wealthy looking person carrying Bible, and a destitute pauper.
3. Aeroplane with words 'Forewarned is forearmed' and in small letters underneath ROYAL OBSERVER CORPS.
4. A picture representing the devil.
5. The words 'They demanded their RIGHTS' and a pair of traditional scales with the world weighing down one side, and God's love in a heart shape in the upper pan.

6. The words 'They kept...' with a jar of ink and a quill pen sticking out and accounts on a scroll with 12 hours, 9, 6, 3, 1—one under another.

(Acetates 5 and 6 could be paired, the former being at the top of a sheet and the latter being on half a sheet attached to the lower left-hand edge and being flipped over when required.)

7. The words 'They grumbled—see Philippians 4:11–13'.
8. The words 'They were...' and the picture of a face completely green except for the hair and eye space.

(Acetates 7 and 8 could be paired similarly to 5 and 6.)

9. The words (placed down the left-hand side of the acetate) 'They accused the owner of injustice'.
10. A picture of Jesus hanging from the cross and the text at the bottom 1 Peter 2:22–24 (to be placed on the right-hand side of the acetate).

PRESENTATION

Ask whether anyone has said or thought this recently at school, home or work. (Acetate 1 on OHP screen.) Even if the parable of the labourers has been read as the Lesson, briefly recap the story and point out that the money mentioned would be roughly a fair day's wage of a labourer to keep him and his family alive for a day. The first labourers agreed to this. The later labourers agreed to no fixed amount, but trusted the owner would pay a fair wage. Ask why the last were paid first. (If they had not been, there would have been no story, because the first would not have known that the last were paid the same as them.)

1. Life does not seem fair (Acetate 2)

Point out that we do live in a world where there seems to be great unfairness: some, like most of us here, have food, homes and money to spare, and we have heard about the Lord Jesus.

Others have none of these things. (Perhaps refer to the latest TV pictures of starving millions, flood victims, etc.)

(a) If we don't believe in God there is no point in complaining that life's unfair, because there is no one to whom we can complain.

(b) If we do believe, then there is the real problem of envy, and two Psalms warn of this—37 and 73—perhaps quote bits. The Royal Observer Corps, which did so much to help win the Battle of Britain in 1940, have as their motto 'Forewarned is forearmed' (acetate 3), so we need to be aware that a very busy devil will (acetate 4) do his best to make us envious.

2. Those complaining workers

Make the following points fairly briefly:

(a) *They demanded their rights* (Acetate 5) and got them, namely a fair day's wage, whereas the others trusted God and discovered him loving and gracious.

(b) *They kept accounts* (Acetate 6). Why should those who only worked one hour get the same? But in fact those who had the shorter hours would no doubt have been pleased to work longer had they been given the chance, and they still had the same needs, namely themselves and their family to keep. (The Editor confesses to his shame that he remembers privately complaining in his heart that he had had all the work to do preparing for a televised Family Service, whereas others taking part had very little to do, yet he and they all got the same fees. He knew he should have been pleased, for his stipend was greater than theirs, but initially he wasn't!)

(c) *They grumbled* (Acetate 7). Mention how God was not pleased with the Children of Israel, when they did the same. By contrast listen to how the Apostle Paul reacted when he was quite unfairly put in prison. Have Philippians 4:11–13 read here.

(d) *They were jealous*. Put on acetate 8 and ask what the congregation think it means. Refer to Miriam in the Old Testament and the Elder Brother in the New Testament as other examples of jealousy. Point out what a fruitless sin jealousy is. We can get some pleasure from pride or lust, etc, but jealousy brings no pleasure, does not help our situation and discourages God's grace towards us.

(e) *They accused the owner of injustice* (Acetate 9). Refer to the woman of uncertain age who demanded of her photographer justice. To which he replied that it was not justice she needed, but mercy! These men were quite wrong, because they got justice, namely exactly what had been agreed. Place acetate 10 on the screen and have 1 Peter 2:22–24 read.

You could finish with the story of John Charles Ryle, Oxford cricket Blue, anticipating a First in his degree, sauntering late into Morning Prayer one Sunday early in 1838 just in time to hear the Second Lesson from Ephesians 2 being read with an air of the most impressive earnestness, especially the eighth verse—'FOR BY GRACE...ARE YE SAVED... THROUGH FAITH...AND THAT...NOT OF YOUR-SELVES...IT IS THE GIFT OF GOD.' Not till that moment, for all his classical scholarship and other attainments, had he ever rightly grasped the gospel of grace and salvation. Later he went on to become the first Bishop of Liverpool. (From *John Charles Ryle 1816–1900* by Marcus L. Loane [James Clarke], 1953, pp 13–14.)

Does everyone here know the grace of God that he found?

Michael Botting
Editor

60   What Happens When We Die?

TEXT

Mark 5:39. 'Not dead, but asleep.'

READING

Mark 5:21–24, 35–43.

PREPARATION

Prepare three simple cut-out outline figures, about 18″ high, and of bright coloured paper.

Jairus' daughter   Jesus   Ourselves

Prepare three cut-out circles of yellow coloured paper, and draw a simple smiling face on each (as far as possible each should be identical).

Prepare six eyes looking upwards, (viz ◖).

Punch a hole at the top of each figure, and in the centre of each eye, including the smiling faces, so that each can be displayed on a blackboard with pins hammered in to support the outline cut-outs. Each figure should have a smiling face beneath it, and, at the bottom of the board, a card with the words 'not dead, but asleep'.

(*Note:* Teazlegraph, Velcro, or double-sided sellotape can also be used, but pins and punched holes are cheap and always to hand, and the outlines can easily be removed and replaced during the talk.)

PRESENTATION

A story of three people. (Hold the outline figures high for all to see.)

1. A little girl (place the figure on the board)

We don't know her name. She was twelve years old, and her father's name was Jairus. Tell the story of Jairus coming to Jesus in his need. A matter of life and death: not a moment to be wasted. But Jesus delayed over a woman who had been ill for twelve years. Then word came that it was too late: the little girl had died. Jairus' heart must have sunk. Tell of Jesus' reply, and coming to Jairus' house. Describe the scene about the door. Jesus said she is *not dead, but asleep* (verse 39). (Display the words at the bottom of the board.) They laughed at him. (Hang a smiling face below the little girl, hung by pins

244

through the eye-holes.) Tell of the little girl being raised to life again. Those who mocked must have seen no miracle: they saw the girl alive and said, 'Well, she *must* have been asleep, but we could have sworn she was dead!' In fact, she *was* dead: but those like the parents who had the eyes of faith (hook a couple of eyes looking upward on the smiling face), saw death transformed: to them, it was a miracle. When Jesus spoke of 'sleep' in relation to death, he spoke only of an *'awakening'* (cf Lazarus, John 11:11). Explain the difference between being dead and being asleep: both look the same, but when you are dead you stay that way; when you are asleep, you wake up sometime. This little girl woke up! Hence 'not dead, but asleep'!

2. *Jesus* (place the next figure on the board, beside the last)

The greater part of the gospel story speaks of Jesus' death. The Service of Holy Communion reminds us of his death: his body broken and his blood shed for us. Jesus was dead. But no! Not dead, but asleep! He came alive again (cf 1 Corinthians 15:20. NB reference to sleep). The fact of the Resurrection is at the heart of the gospel, and was the basis of the Apostles' preaching in the Acts.

When Paul came to Athens (Acts 17) and spoke of the Resurrection, some mocked (display the smiling face); and some believed (add the eyes looking upward in faith) (verses 32–34). 1 Corinthians 15 speaks of all those who *saw* Jesus alive: Paul is saying, 'Go and ask them for yourself: most of them are still alive, but some have fallen asleep' (NB that word!). There is a sense in which Jesus, then, was 'not dead, but asleep'—for he awoke from death, and rose to new life.

3. *Ourselves* (place the third figure on the board)

What happens when we die? A question many are asking. Some laugh (place the smiling figure on the board) and say, 'When you're dead, you're finished! Death is the end.' But to the eye of faith, which looks up and trusts the Lord Jesus, it is once again 'not dead, but asleep': Christians don't die (John 11:25–26. NB *'never die'*, cf the Funeral Service); they *sleep* (cf 1 Thessalonians 4:13ff and 1 Corinthians 15), i.e. they look forward to an awakening. For a Christian, death is abolished (2 Timothy 1:10), transformed. Just as we are not afraid to go to sleep at night, trusting that we will wake in the morning, so Christians believe that death is but a sleep from which we will one day awaken. When we wake up, we will find ourselves with Jesus, and what could be better than that? 'Not dead, but asleep' is true of those whose eyes are lifted in faith to Jesus (the word 'cemetery' comes from the Greek word 'to sleep').

Remember, this figure represents you and me: what do *you* think happens when we die? Are you like those who laugh and mock, saying 'Impossible!'—or do you have the eyes of faith which look at death and say with confidence, 'Not dead, but asleep!'?

Theological footnote

It is needless to consider (as many do) in what sense the word 'sleep' refers to the body or the spirit after death, whether it is conscious or unconscious sleep. This is to miss the point entirely: for Jesus and the Apostle Paul this was never the issue. Wherever we read of 'sleep' in the New Testament in relation to death, the sole fact is being expressed that death is not the end; rather, *an awakening* is to be expected. The purpose of this talk is to convey the same simple truth. Not dead, but asleep.

Stephen Trapnell
Marlborough

Bible Characters

61 Jesus Christ—His Baptism According to Matthew

TEXT

Matthew 3.

AIM

To show how Jesus' baptism is an acted parable of his mission of salvation.

PREPARATION

Make four large cards with the following words on them:

(a) Sinful
(b) Unworthy
(c) Sinless
(d) Acceptable to God

PRESENTATION

This talk can be used either at a suitable occasion prior to the service (eg in Sunday school), or at the beginning of the service, or at the beginning of a longer talk.

Present the following riddle:

A man is found guilty of murder and is awaiting the judge's sentence. He has confessed his guilt; he was caught in the very act of a premeditated killing. He shows no remorse and is completely sane. There were absolutely no mitigating circumstances (explain, if necessary!). He was not a member of the armed forces, or acting under orders, duress of any kind, or indeed hypnosis. The judge pronounced sentence as follows: 'You have been found guilty of murder. The only penalty I can give is life-imprisonment, but in view of your special condition I have no option but to let you go a free man.' Why was this the case? What was the man's special condition?

At this point do not ask for any suggestions, but go through the story of Jesus' baptism making the following points.

1. John's baptism was a baptism of repentance.
2. John was Jesus' cousin—so they knew each other.
3. Water in baptism symbolises the washing away of sins.
4. Jesus joined the queue with all the others to be baptised by John.
5. John recognised Jesus and protested that Jesus should baptise him.
6. Jesus insisted on being baptised by John.
7. The Spirit of God confirms Jesus as Messiah.
8. What does it all mean?

Explain

    (a) Jesus is one with us.
    (b) We have forgiveness and eternal life through union with Christ.

Ask for volunteers to hold up the cards as you refer to them.

1. First, we are SINFUL and need to repent.
2. So we are UNWORTHY of heaven, and because we are sinful we cannot ever fully repent.
3. Jesus was SINLESS. He has done nothing for which he needs to repent.
4. Jesus is God's beloved Son so he is ACCEPTABLE TO GOD.

Now, what's the solution? Ask for an answer to the riddle—the convicted man was a Siamese twin!

If someone has guessed this, then explain that so it is with us and Jesus: being a Christian means being united with Christ—being joined to him spiritually like a Siamese twin. 'When anyone is united to Christ he is a new creature: his old life is over; a new life has already begun' (2 Corinthians 5:17, NEB).

If we are joined to Jesus then we escape punishment for our sins because God says: 'Any friend of Jesus is a friend of mine.'

Next make children with SINFUL and SINLESS cards stand right up next to each other; and likewise children with UNWORTHY and ACCEPTABLE TO GOD cards.

If nobody has guessed the riddle, then get the children with the cards to stand together as explained above—the answer should then be forthcoming! Then talk about being united with Christ.

Conclude by summing up that 'being joined to Christ' is well expressed in the phrase 'that we may evermore dwell in him and he in us'.

David McIntosh
Ellesmere Port

62 Jesus Christ—His Baptism According to John

TEXT

John 1:29–34.

AIM

To explain John's teaching about Jesus.

PREPARATION

Half fill a large black bin liner with garden leaves or other domestic rubbish which will be heavy but not sharp to rip the liner! Prepare a washing up bowl with water, a flannel and a towel, and a jug of water with two glasses. Have a large cross which you can erect or bring on when required.

PRESENTATION

John the Baptist's ministry prepared the way for Jesus. He called him:

1. *The Lamb of God who takes away the sin of the world (v 29)*

   Get two or three children to try to carry the bin liner. Carry it yourself. Explain how you get your garden rubbish taken away. But the rubbish inside our hearts (eg selfishness, disobedience) Jesus has taken so that we can be forgiven and freed from our burden (drop the bag).

2. *The One who baptises with the Holy Spirit (v 33b)*

Ask for a volunteer to have a wash. When you have washed and dried a face, explain that John was washing/baptising people as a sign that they were sorry and wanted to be made clean from their sins. But Jesus would do something much greater than that. Ask for another volunteer and offer a glass of soapy water from the washing up bowl. Why is it refused? That water won't do much good to your inside! Offer instead a glass of fresh water from the jug. Jesus offers to reach right inside us and pour God's Spirit into our hearts. But like the glass of water that has been offered, *we* have to drink!

3. *The Son of God (v 34)*

Set up the large cross. John recognised that it could not be just a man who would do these things. 'He existed before I was born' (v 30b). He has all power and authority as Son of God, even though he humbly awaits our response to his offer of forgiveness through the cross and the gift of his Spirit.

Ted Crofton
Cheltenham

63   Jesus Christ—His Transfiguration

TEXT

Luke 9:28–43.

AIM

To explain the meaning of the Transfiguration.

PREPARATION

The visual aid consists of a flannelgraph board showing a hill. It needs to be able to hold six vertical fluorescent strips, approximately 6″ by 1″. Card is best for easy handling. They should be in different colours, one being white (with glitter) and slightly larger than the others, to make it stand out. You may also want extra strips to represent the crowd at the bottom of the hill.

PRESENTATION

1. The Vision

This is what the disciples saw.

As the events are unfolded, so the strips are put on to the hill vertically. First Jesus (in white to represent his glory, 2 Peter 1:17–18), then the disciples, then the two Old Testament characters, one on either side. Show how the two represented the Law and the Prophets, and that they both pointed forward to Christ's coming death on the cross, and his Resurrection (verse 31). Old Testament passages can be used to support this. The confirmation and encouragement Christ received. The fact that both the Law and the Prophets were fulfilled in Christ.

2. *The Voice*

This is what the disciples heard.

Continue the story and show how Peter sought to put Jesus on the same level as Moses and Elijah by building all three a place of adoration. But at the crucial moment there was before them Jesus only (remove two of the strips). The voice, similar to that at his baptism, confirms his Person and his authority. This is one of the main points of the Transfiguration. Stress this—the incomparable Jesus.

3. *The Valley*

This is what they did.

The disciples would probably have liked to stay there and hear more, but they had to go down into the daily round again and take what they had seen and heard into their everyday experience. So it should be with our worship and witness. You could have a number of strips at the bottom of the mountain and mingle the others with them, asking those present what sort of things they would say to the people they met.

Donald Churchman
Hayling Island

253

64   Jesus Christ—At Prayer

TEXTS

Mark 14:36, referring also to John 8:29 and Matthew 6:9–13.

AIM

To show some principles of pleasing God from our Lord's prayers.

PREPARATION

Prepare a card or paper with 'Please God' on it, the letters G, o, d being moveable, so that they can be spelt vertically. Prepare three other cards with the part words 'lorify him', 'bey him' and 'epend on him'.

   Three pictures can also be used, either cut from magazines or drawn with simple figures. (1) Proud father congratulating award-winning son in front of a football goal. (2) Tall boy mowing lawn, with father beside him and swimming gear—flippers, towel, snorkel, etc—behind him. (3) Large dog pulling small boy, man behind boy reaching over with arm.

PRESENTATION

Has anybody done something for another person today, or this week? You took your wife breakfast in bed? You cooked your son's favourite dish? And they said 'Thank you very much.' Most of us are glad when we've pleased someone. Jesus always pleased his Father (John 8:29). (Put up 'Please God'.) Whatever he did it pleased God. Our aim is to do the same, so if we copy Jesus we know we will please God.

Jesus prayed. He talked with God early, alone and with others there. He didn't just ask, he shared his plans, joys, disappointments. He thanked him.

1. *Who likes football?* Anybody's dad a footballer? If you do well he's proud of you, and people say, 'He's a credit to his father' (put up picture 1). In other words you glorify him. (Take the 'G' and put it below, and to the right of the 'Please', and add the rest of 'lorify him'.) When Jesus did anything he glorified God. He included the idea in the Lord's Prayer, 'Hallowed be thy name.'

2. *Anyone's dad ask them to do something* this week when they wanted to do something different? Jesus learned to obey his Father—have you? You wanted to go swimming (picture 2), but Dad said, 'Not till you've mown the lawn.' Jesus called God 'Abba', which means 'Dad' ('Daddy', 'Pop', 'Papa'—whichever word seems apt for the audience), and Paul says God has given us the same Spirit so that we can talk to him in the same way. But that means we must also say 'Thy will be done.' (Put up 'bey him'.)

3. *Who's got a dog?* Big one? Do you find he's a bit big to hold sometimes? This boy did (picture 3), he needed help and strength. Jesus needed help often, and he came to his Father for it. He asked for guidance in difficult decisions. He asked for courage to face suffering. He depended on God. So you and I need to depend on him (put up 'epend on him'). You see, the boy has asked his father to take over the situation, and his strong hand has come over the boy's.

So in the Lord's Prayer we say, 'Give us bread...deliver us...'

Conclusion

You want to please God? Then please glorify him, please obey him and please depend on him.

Peter Barton
Malmesbury

65   Noah—The Three Doors

Texts

Genesis 7:16; John 10:9; Revelation 3:20 (GNB).

Aim

To tell the story of Noah and the Flood in order to speak of God's justice, love and invitation to faith.

Preparation

You will need an OHP with three prepared acetate sheets. On sheet one draw a simple landscape of hills, trees, fields, etc (it is important that you use water-based pens for this). Prepare sheet two as shown, with a cardboard cross and opening door stuck to the acetate, and the text John 10:9 on overlays, but cutting out a gap over the door. Sheet three is prepared as sheet two but with a card heart and opening door and the text Revelation 3:20 surrounding the heart with the words 'I will come in' beneath the door. You will also need a card cut-out of an ark, with an opening door, and a card cut-out with the word 'sin'. The card shows as a silhouette when projected on the screen. You will also need a glass of water and a set of water-based OHP pens with you.

Begin by asking someone to look up Genesis 1:31 and read it aloud. Show visual one and ask for two volunteers to come and add to God's beautiful world. Ask the congregation to judge if the picture is good. Go on to explain how things soon changed and that the people God had created out of love soon rebelled against him.

Ask someone to read Genesis 6:5–7 and explain that God looked at the world again, but this time didn't like what he saw and that verse 6 is one of the saddest verses in the Bible. Because God cannot tolerate evil he had to put an end to it, and so he decided to make it rain. (Taking great care, flick a few drops of water onto the acetate and then wipe the picture away, explaining verse 7.) What a waste of a beautiful picture! But then what a waste of God's beautiful world. Go on to explain that the root of evil is sin (place silhouette card with 'sin' over the smudged picture).

God looked again and found one man who was different. Noah's desire was obedience to God and so God rescued him and his family. Ask someone to read Genesis 6:8–14 and 16b—7:1.

1. God's door of justice

Replace the silhouette 'sin' with the 'ark' (keeping the door open). Explain how difficult it must have been for Noah to please God in a world that has rebelled against him, and draw the parallels with Christians living in today's world. Noah and his family obeyed God by entering the ark and *God closed the door* (7:16). Explain that God made the decision to separate good from evil by closing the door on the sin that had entered his world. Then the rain came. (Ask congregation to tap one finger against their other hand, then two fingers, and so on, until they all clap their hands together. This creates the sound of rain very effectively!) God had pronounced his judgement. Explain that Noah wasn't perfect, but because of his obedience to God

Visual 1

Visual 2

"Listen! I stand at the door... and knock..."

"I will Come in"

Revelation ch. 3 verse 20

Visual 3

"I am the door... Whoever comes in by me will be saved"

John ch.10 verse 9

Overlay for Visual 2 — cut acetate along broken lines.

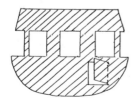

he was saved. (Ask the congregation if they know which man was perfect, and get them to say Jesus.)

2. *God's door of love*

What can we learn from the story of Noah? We aren't in danger of coming under God's judgement by another worldwide flood (Genesis 8:21), but there is still *this* to be dealt with (replace smudged picture and ark with silhouette 'sin'). Explain that God's door of justice is still closed on the world because of man's sin, but God is also a God of love and he has opened another door for us. (Display visual two with door open.) Explain that just as God had a plan to save Noah, so too he has a plan to save us. (Display John 10:9 by overlaying the flaps.) Explain that just as Noah demonstrated his trust in God's plan to save him by going through the door of the ark, so we too must demonstrate our trust in God's plan to save us by accepting Jesus' invitation of love. It may seem simple and even stupid, but that's what the people of Noah's day thought of the ark! (See 1 Corinthians 1:18–19.) Ask the congregation if they have walked through God's door of love. Tell them that just as God closed the door of the ark, there is a day coming when God will close this door too.

3. *God's door of invitation*

Display visual three with door of heart closed and explain that the Bible talks of a third door. The first door God closed, the second door God opened, but this door we have complete control over, either to open or keep shut. But if we decide to open the door of our hearts to God, he can be trusted to keep his promise, 'I will come in,' just as he did with Noah.

Bob Kiteley
Chester

66 Abraham—At Prayer

TEXT

Genesis 18 and 19.

AIM

To teach some principles of intercessory prayer.

PREPARATION

Draw three basic backgrounds on paper as illustrated:
   (1) Valley of the Jordan with city (Sodom) in middle distance and Dead Sea beyond;
   (2) Plateau with nomadic tent on right;
   (3) front of Eastern-type house.
   You will also need: (4) picture of TV with 'credits'. Draw some 'match-stick' figures: (5) Abraham sitting; (6) Abraham standing, looking left; (7) Abraham prone, head left; (8) three men walking right; (9) two men walking left; (10) man standing, pointing left. Four phrases on card or paper 'Make friends with God', 'Be friends with others', 'Pray for your friends', 'God answers prayer'.

Ask who watched TV yesterday. You may have seen at the end of a programme a list of people who helped present it—credits (put up picture 4). Everyone is important, not just the actors. *You* are important to this church and in God's family.

This service can't go on without organist, wardens, reader, sidesmen, cleaners, etc, and those who put money in collection to pay for heat and light, etc, and most important all who pray that God will bless us. Producer of programme perhaps the most important but you never see him. One Christian needs the prayers of other Christians as he is preaching, singing in the choir or reading the lesson.

1. Abraham made friends with God

Abraham was called 'the friend of God' because he believed God and obeyed him. He had established a relationship with God. But you and I can be friends of God if we accept Jesus as Saviour. Jesus said 'You are my friends...' Abraham had a nephew, Lot. For a time they had lived together in a tent like this (picture 2) but as time went on both their families had grown and they decided to separate. Describe Abraham's kindness in giving Lot the choice. Lot chose the valley (picture 1, if possible adjacent to picture 2). A dangerous choice because Sodom people were cruel and wicked.

2. Abraham made friends with others

Abraham prayed often for Lot's safety and was ready for God to use him if necessary. Once he had to rescue him after he had been taken prisoner by an enemy army. One day Abraham was sitting (picture 5) by his tent when three travellers approached (picture 8); he stood to welcome them (picture 6) and bowed low (picture 7). Mention briefly meal and conversation (if time). One of the three was God himself—revealed in human form—as later Jesus was. God began to talk about Sodom's wickedness and sent off the other two men (picture 9). The Bible says they were angels. (Then put picture 6 and picture 10 overlooking valley.)

3. *Abraham prayed for his friends*

Abraham is very concerned about Lot and prays for him and the city. Describe the 'count down' (verses 23–32). Ask if any of congregation have burden to pray for someone.

4. *Abraham's prayer was answered*

God listened to his prayer and told the angels to take Lot and his family out of Sodom (picture 3 and superimpose two angels, picture 9). God does answer your prayers for others. He wants you to be willing to help but he may keep you in the background, and use someone else actually to minister to them. Everyone is important. So pray for your friends. Remember the TV programme (picture 4), and give God the credit for what he does through his people.

Depending on your audience you could at some point conclude the story by explaining that God had to destroy the city because of the extreme wickedness of the people, but this was also showing mercy on the children, to save them growing up in such a terrible environment. He did, however, answer Abraham's prayer for Lot.

Peter Barton
Malmesbury

67 Joseph

TEXT

Genesis 37:2–11.

AIM

To show some of the causes and the remedy for hatred in the family, using the early life of Joseph as an example.

PREPARATION

1. Write up the three words:

> Favouritism   Pride   Jealousy

2. Obtain a large torch with two batteries—one expired, one new.

PRESENTATION

Introduction

The story of Joseph is one of the most exciting stories in the whole Bible. Here we read of dreams with hidden meanings, of prison in enemy hands, of being sold as a slave, of trust as a ruler by the king himself, of disguises from his own family, of journeys in time of famine, of hostages and ransom money, of arrests and reunions, of presents and gifts including 'twenty donkeys laden with good things'!

First meeting with Joseph

When we first meet Joseph he is surrounded by angry and jealous brothers. He had ten older brothers, and his father Jacob was a very rich man with hundreds of sheep on land which stretched for mile after mile. But all their happiness was spoilt by anger, for his brothers hated Joseph. Anger and hatred are still qualities which make for unhappiness in families.

Why were they angry?

No one person in the family was to blame; they were all guilty.

(a) *The father.* Jacob, or Israel as he came to be called, loved all his children; but he specially loved Joseph. We read how he gave him a coat of many colours, or a coat of long sleeves. Here was a coat fit for a king, certainly not for the youngest son!

Here was the first cause of hatred in the family—the favouritism of the father (show word on card).

How right he was in loving his children, but how wrong he was in having a favourite. (Read verse 4 aloud.)

(b) *Joseph himself.* He was to blame because of the proud way in which he told his dream to his brothers. Of course there was nothing wrong in having a dream! What was wrong was the way in which he told it (show second word on card). You will remember his two dreams (read 37:5–11). He told them with pride, and this made his brothers jealous (NB verse 8).

How easy but wrong it is, when we know we are better than someone else at a job or a sport, to boast about it!

(c) *The brothers.* They too were to blame. It was no excuse to say that their brother had provoked them to be jealous (show third word on card).

So each member of the family was to blame.

What about a remedy?

We could all think of quick remedies which might have solved the immediate problem; the father should have been more loving, Joseph should have been humble and the brothers should have happily shared in their youngest brother's dream.

It's easier to put the remedy into words than to put it into deeds! In all probability the family knew what they should have done. The father Jacob certainly knew that favouritism led to hatred (his own father and mother had had favourites when he was a boy; it caused such unhappiness that in the end he had to run away from home).

Illustration of a torch

It is rather like this torch which will not shine. Just cleaning the glass on the outside will make no difference, nor will shaking help! It is only mended when you take out the old battery and put in a new one. (Do just that with the torch.)

So with us. It is no good just trying to be more loving, more humble, more content to share; we must first get to the root cause of the matter, and, as it were, put in a new battery. It is the battery which will enable us to do what we know we should be doing. Paul speaks of this in Romans 7:19 when he writes: 'For I do not do the good I want, but the evil I do not want is what I do.' And he goes on, 'Who will deliver me...? Thanks be to God, through our Lord Jesus Christ!'

Paul acknowledges that in the end it is only as he has the strength that comes from the Lord Jesus Christ that he will be able to do what he knows he should. It is as though Jesus Christ were himself the new battery we need.

This will mean telling the Lord Jesus that we have done wrong; it will mean asking his forgiveness; and it will mean constantly seeking to live not in our own strength but in the strength which only comes from him.

Other talks could be worked out in a series on Joseph, eg Genesis 37:19–36, showing how one sin leads to another, and Genesis 39:1–6, showing that God never leaves us alone, even though we may be in a strange place, with strange people, and a strange religion.

Garry Guinness
Worthing

68 Moses

Texts

Exodus 2:1–10; Hebrews 11:23–26; Acts 7:20–29.

Aim

To show that God gives us opportunities and the strength to use them.

Preparation

Prepare some pictures: (1) front of palace, (2) match-stick figures of man and woman standing, looking right, (3) basket in reeds at river's edge, (4) girl looking right, (5) princess, standing, looking left—(2), (3), (4) and (5) to make up one picture. Pictures of (6) car and (7) church.

Prepare three cards with the words: 'Relationships', 'Resources' and 'Renunciation'.

Presentation

Do you always take opportunities when you should? A schoolboy returned to school for prizegiving a year after leaving; he had not worked very hard at school and so he had had difficulty getting a job at all, let alone an interesting one. 'I wish I'd made the most of my opportunities.'

A woman had the offer of a free cookery course before she married, but felt she had not the time. Later she wished she had made the most of her opportunities.

Moses was a great man in the court of Pharaoh (picture 1). I believe his greatness came at least partly from his taking his opportunities.

1. His relationships

Note first his relationships. He was a Hebrew, son of a slave, but he became a member of the royal family. Remember Joseph? He'd come to Egypt as a slave, but through God's miraculous work, Joseph had brought prosperity to the country. Some 350 years later a Pharaoh came to the throne who didn't know Joseph and didn't want to know his Hebrew descendants. So he made them slaves and said: 'Reduce their number, throw the babies into the river.'

Moses had godly parents (2), who committed him to God in a—what? Yes, a waterproofed basket (3). His brave sister cared for him (4) till he was adopted by—who? Yes, the princess (5).

2. *His resources*

Have you ever tried playing golf with only a driver or tried to drive a car (6) without brakes or petrol? You must have some basic resources or supplies of essentials. Moses started well with *beauty* before God (Acts 7:20). God had chosen him and made him attractive (to encourage his parents to try to save him perhaps?). He found *wisdom* through his education in Egypt (Acts 7:22) (are you making the most of your education?). Moses was *mighty* in words and deeds (Acts 7:22). He knew how to speak and act with power and effectiveness. He even had *wealth*, far beyond his needs. God will supply all your needs from his infinite resources. Are you making the most of all your resources?

3. *His renunciation*

In spite of all this Moses made his renunciation. He gave up his claim to the fame and to the wealth and materialism of Egypt (Hebrews 11:24–25), choosing rather to identify himself with God's people (as you are now doing in church) (7). An athlete may have to renounce his freedom to live a life of indulgence if he wants to win a prize.

Conclusion

Moses made the most of his opportunities and God used him to bring his people out of slavery into their own land. You may not be called upon to do anything like that, but God gives us all opportunities of various kinds. Pray that he will help you to see them and to make the most of them.

Peter Barton
Malmesbury

69 Miriam

Text

Exodus 2:1–10.

Aim

To show that no human life is immune from the threat of jealousy; how to avoid it; how to get right, through Christ, if overcome by it.

Preparation

Prepare pictures as shown below.

Presentation

Scene 1: A daring sister

Tell the story of Miriam's courage when Moses was three months old. Sketch in all that depended upon the safety of that baby (i.e. the law, the prophets, civilisation as we know it, floating in embryo down the river in a frail basket). But around the baby, a family's faith, a sister's determination, the unseen protecting love of God.

Scene 2: An inspiring leader

Miriam next appears in Exodus 15:20–21. The Great Escape

has just taken place! The children of Israel have just passed through the Red Sea, and the pursuing Egyptian forces have been drowned. Jubilant, the Israelites celebrate on the far shore...and there is Miriam, leading the singing and worship of the women folk, dancing before them.

Miriam, though overshadowed by her famous brothers, has found a role of her own. Although unmarried, she is finding fulfilment in leadership among the women. Her record is further polished!

Scene 3: A jealous rival

The next mention of Miriam is not until Numbers 12. All has not been well with Miriam for some time, and now it boils over. She criticises Moses for marrying a Cushite woman— presumably Zipporah, whose Midianite ancestry made her a Cushite. And coloured.

Very likely this was just a pretext. After all, Zipporah had been around for a long time. Beware of inventing reasons for criticism! But soon Miriam's real reason became public. She was envious of Moses. 'Huh! Why him? Why not me? Hasn't the Lord prophesied through me as well as that stuck-up brother of mine?' She infected her weak-willed brother Aaron with the same poisonous resentment.

Jealousy is a strange and ugly condition. If you hoard gold bars under the bed, or vainly regard your face as the most beautiful in the northern hemisphere, you get some pleasure from your pride, but there is no such compensation in jealousy. It eats up the person who suffers from it. Jealousy comes from the wrong kind of comparison. The lads who kick a football around our park may not feel a twinge of jealousy towards their favourite football star—but they may towards each other when teams are chosen. We are most open to jealousy towards people in our own immediate circle, and even noble Miriam was no exception. Indeed, no one is immune, not politicians, not teachers, not doctors, not missionaries, not clergy, not church members.

The remedy

1. Admit it to yourself. Be honest and face it. What, *me*? Jealous? Yes, you! Almost everyone is likely to experience it at times. Some people seem to suffer from it all the time. It spoils all their pleasure.

2. Recognise its seriousness. It is harmful to you, injurious to others. Jealousy caused Saul to try and murder David; it led directly to the crucifixion of Jesus: 'Pilate knew it was for jealousy the Jews delivered him up.' It will eat your character and destroy all the pleasure you have in what you *have* got.

3. Recognise its seriousness in God's sight. Read what severe words God had to say to Miriam, as recorded in Numbers 12.

4. Get rid of it as quickly as possible! Jealousy is like dirty bathwater—pull out the plug and get rid of it.

5. How? Stop being envious of the other person's good fortune, success, skill, beauty or whatever it is. Instead, *pray* for that person, and ask God to bless them. Ask God to cleanse your heart of such ugly bitterness, and thank him for that person's talents and qualities. If necessary, pray the same prayer 150 times, until you are cured.

Don't let *your* character be disfigured by the sin that blotted Miriam's record.

John Simons
Nailsea, Bristol

70 Joshua

Joshua 1:1–5, 5:13–15.

AIM

To teach God's continued presence and available strength.

PREPARATION

(1) You can use the same picture as for the talk on the Trinity (No. 33), 'Spaghetti Junction' or a drawing of something else that is fairly complicated. (2) Pictures of walled town with hills behind; (3) office—pram—school; (4) match-stick man bowing to ground before another standing holding sword; (5) burning bush.

Prepare cards or strips of paper with paragraph headings to stick up as appropriate.

What is this? Show (1), Spaghetti Junction or your own choice of a complicated problem. Fairly perplexing, but not if you know where you are going, look at the instructions and go ahead.

Joshua, commander of Israeli land forces, directed to occupy Palestine. Facing first major problem—impregnable Jericho (2). He felt inadequate. He had managed in the desert but this was different. Moses was not there to help any longer. He was on his own. Do you feel like that sometimes? Are you facing responsibility—a new job with large staff—first baby—being a prefect at school? (show pictures if you like) (3).

1. *Be assured of God's presence*

'As I was with Moses, so I will be with you' (Joshua 1:5). You are not on your own—God is with you. Jesus said the same, 'I am with you always' (Matthew 28:20). I was and I will be because I AM. 'I AM' is his name and his nature.

2. *Be attentive to God's promises*

As he looked at the problem Joshua almost forgot God's promises, 'The land I am giving them' (1:2). Then he saw a man (4) with a drawn sword (5:13). 'Friend or foe?' 'The Captain of the Lord's army.' Joshua fell down and worshipped. (Did he feel a fool, falling down before he had checked the man's credentials—was he a Canaanite spy?) 'What are your commands?' (probably expected a long list of difficult instructions). 'Take off your shoes.' That was easy! That rings a bell. It was what God said to Moses by the burning bush (5). 'So it *is* God speaking—the great I AM confirming his promises to me.' Read the commands and promises in the Bible frequently and act on them. God was with Moses all right—and now he is with you. His command contained his promise.

3. Be expectant of God's power

As God made a way through the Red Sea, so he would make a way into Jericho, and he did. And so he will make a way through for you—and give you strength and wisdom for your responsibility.

Conclusion

Know his presence, look at his promises and go ahead in his power.

Peter Barton
Malmesbury

71 Samuel

TEXTS

1 Samuel 1:1–20, 3:1–10, 7:7–13a, 16:1–13.

AIM

To show the possibility of communication between God and man; the desire on God's part for this; the reality in Samuel's experience.

PREPARATION

Tell the story briefly, with salient points only. Attention can be focused by using one or two large flannelgraph figures for each story. As the talk proceeds build up the following:

God heard	*Samuel heard*
Hannah's prayer	God's call
Samuel's prayer	God's instructions

You will also need a radio, a record and a whistle.

PRESENTATION

Point of contact

Who likes talking? In school—in bed at night—etc? Do you like listening? To this (radio) or this (record)? Here is something which tells you what to do (show referee's whistle). It is as well to listen to its instructions! Two things we all do—talk and listen. A pleasure—but very useful too!

1. *Someone talking*—asking for something (1 Samuel 1:9–12— refer back to reason, verse 6). Who is she talking to? The Lord (verse 10). Did God hear (verse 20)? 'Samuel' means 'heard of the Lord'. Do you talk to God? Ask for things as Hannah did? God always hears. Sometimes he says 'yes'. At other times 'no' or 'wait a while'.

2. *Does God talk to us?* Tell story in 1 Samuel 3:1–10. Samuel wasn't expecting God to speak. He couldn't hear properly at first because he wasn't really listening. Some people find it hard to hear—deaf—need hearing-aid. So did Samuel— Eli was his 'hearing-aid'. God wants to talk to us all—we need to listen—we may need a hearing-aid (the Bible, a hymn, the advice of an older Christian). God was calling Samuel to be a follower of his, and to work for him as he grew older.

3. *Samuel grew up*—became leader of the people. One day they were in great trouble (1 Samuel 7:7–13a). Samuel cried to God—God heard him (verse 9). Samuel knew what to do—as his mother had done! Had she taught him?

   Do you have to do piano practice, football practice, etc? When we practise we learn to do things better. Remember how the boy Samuel found it hard to recognise God's voice? He got better at hearing it as years went by. Tell story in brief (1 Samuel 16:1–13). Samuel heard and obeyed God's instructions (like instructions given by referee's whistle).

Conclusion

We are probably better at *talking to God* than *listening to him*. He very much wants to talk to us—we have to 'tune-in' to him (demonstrate on radio).

Garth Grinham
Southport

72   David

TEXT

2 Samuel 11 and 12.

AIM

To warn of the temptations to immorality, with positive suggestions for avoiding action.

PREPARATION

Prepare a large picture of the front of a palace (1) with parapet. A single picture of a garden (house wall on the right) (2). Prepare head and shoulders of a man (3) looking from parapet towards garden and woman (4). Pictures of ice lolly (5) and bed (6). Prepare words 'Downfall' and 'Climb up' and other headings if desired, especially 'If you can't be good', 'be filled with the Spirit'.

PRESENTATION

David—no saint—mixed up—resentful—vengeful—brutal. A brilliant tactician—an army officer in a million; could have out-manoeuvred modern generals with ten times better equipment, and he didn't go to Sandhurst. He was unbeatable. He was good, or was he? He was a good general, good organiser, good shot with a sling, swordsman, soldier. But he was not a good *man*. At times he *could* not be good. Is it like that for you sometimes? Hard as you try, temptation is just too strong.

Temptation to eat too many sweets or ices (picture 5)
to lie in bed too long (6)
to steal from supermarket
to say unkind word to hurt
to sleep with someone when no one will know.
You fall and feel terrible.

Jesus said: 'Keep my commandments.' We neglect and disobey at our own peril. David didn't know Jesus, but he did know God, and his commandments. He praised God, he trusted God. But note the steps to his...

Downfall

1. Lazed off guard—the devil finds work for idle hands to do (pictures 1 and 3).
2. Looked longingly—house next door (2) and beautiful woman with no bikini (4) (match-stick figure might be wise!)
3. Lusted greedily. 'I want...'
4. Laid plans skilfully—and she wasn't too innocent either—what a compliment to be in the King's favour.
5. Up to the neck! One thing led to another—coveting—adultery—guilt—panic—murder.

How does he get back up again?

Climb up

1. Hear God's word—Nathan
2. Admit guilt   —2 Samuel 12:13
3. Be forgiven   —Believe you are forgiven
4. Suffer patiently   —Consequences of sin are inevitable (2 Samuel 12:15—23)
5. Accept help   —Pray for God's help and ask him to give you the Holy Spirit—the Spirit of Jesus that gave him power to resist

temptation. Let the Holy Spirit have full control of you.

David had Nathan to help him climb up again and the Lord was able to use David again after this episode. You and I have more than David did. We have older Christians and ministers; we have the example and teaching of Jesus; above all we have the Spirit of Jesus to make us holy—if we will let him.

The more you surrender to him the quicker will be your climb up so...

'If you can't be good'—'be filled with the Spirit'.

Peter Barton
Malmesbury

NB This is a difficult subject for a Family Service. For a different approach see *For All The Family* (ed Michael Botting) published by Kingsway, Talk 1, pp 23–25.

73 Nehemiah

TEXT

Nehemiah 1:1—2:8.

AIM

To show some of the conditions necessary for ensuring answers to prayer.

PREPARATION

If possible, get hold of a two-way intercom wireless, telephone or baby's cry detector (someone in the congregation has probably got the latter). Check that it works and try it in church from the pulpit to the vestry or somewhere out of sight. Appoint a stooge to speak to during the service. A simple string with two tin lids can be a good starter.

Draw four pictures of the Nehemiah story. (1) Man talking to Nehemiah and pointing back. (2) Nehemiah kneeling praying. (3) Nehemiah holding cup to king who is looking at him. (4) King pointing and Nehemiah bowing.

Draw four pictures of a rocket. (5) Complete rocket on launching pad. (6) Space capsule going up and right. (7) Space capsule with large gaping hole in the side. (8) Nose cone just above sea.

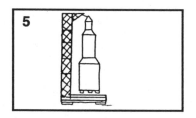

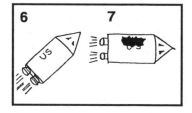

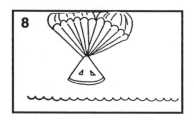

If you like to add headings, prepare four: Make Contact, Check for Mistakes, Maintain the Link, Ask for Help.

Do you sometimes feel that your prayers get no higher than the ceiling? It may be a simple problem of communication. Ever tried a telephone with two tin tops and a long piece of string? It is not very clear, but some sound carries from one end to the other. Ever watched a Water Board official listening to the ground with a long stick? He can usually locate a leaky pipe quite quickly.

1. Make contact

But for speech, a radio link is a lot better. (Hello, are you there?) Brief chat about something amusing or interesting. Then explain how you had to *make contact* first (put up words). Heard of Nehemiah? Great man, but only a servant of the King—his cupbearer, winetaster or butler. But even though he was just a servant he had faith in a great God. He made contact with God, and when news came about the walls of Jerusalem being broken down (picture 1), he straight away talked to God. Do you know Jesus? Come to him and ask him to forgive your mistakes and sins. Ask him to take over your life. That's how to make the first contact.

2. Check for mistakes

When we first tried the radio out in church it didn't work. We found the fault—it needed new batteries. It is always as well to *check for mistakes* and put them right. This is always wise when you come to God. Ask him to remind you of anything in your life that isn't pleasing to him. Then say sorry and ask for forgiveness (picture 2). Nehemiah did this. He confessed his own and his nation's sins.

3. Maintain the link

Nehemiah needed to *maintain the link* with God, reminding himself of some of the great promises of God—to restore the Jews to their own land, etc. If you don't maintain the link with headquarters you may find that just when you are needing help you have lost the link.

Some time ago Apollo 13 had some trouble—you may remember (picture 5). On the launch pad the crew, once inside the capsule, made contact with NASA by radio. They then checked carefully for mistakes. After blast-off they maintained the link (picture 6)—a link with head-quarters which was going to prove vital on their trip.

4. Ask for help

Look ahead to the day—a tricky interview, a bully at school to stand up to, a visit to the dentist, a neighbour who is complaining about your dog—look ahead and link up. Nehemiah linked up each day. Now when the crisis comes you are ready to *ask for help* (picture 3). Nehemiah was sad—a crime then. 'What's up?' 'My home and my people.' 'What do you want?' So he prayed to the God of heaven, and he said to the king, 'Please let me go,' and the king granted him what he asked, because the good hand of God was upon him (picture 4). Apollo 13 had a near disaster (picture 7). Explosion—hole in the side—but radio link held. They asked for help and were given it. They landed safely (picture 8).

God will answer you too if you remember the conditions.

Peter Barton
Malmesbury

74 Jonah (1) Running Away from God

Text

Jonah 1—2.

Aim

To teach about the folly of attempting to run away from God.

Preparation

Ideally obtain a copy of a filmstrip of Jonah, such as that produced by Concordia Publishing House, 28 Huntingdon Road, Cambridge CB3 0HH (0223 65113). CCF 444 covers the whole story. Using suitable members of the congregation produce recorded sound with appropriate sound effects to accompany the filmstrip. This can be used in place of the Lesson. Section 1 Chapter 4 gives details of how this can be done using back projection.

Have the following words available to be shown on an OHP or Teazlegraph board: 'God knows', 'God cares', 'God forgives'. Also have a small cross. If using an OHP the comparison of Jonah with Jesus outlined under Presentation might be shown.

Ask if there are occasions when there are jobs to be done in the house—but you are not to be found. Adults can be no different; we can hide behind agenda paper when chores are being handed out!

Much more seriously God has not put any of us in this world solely for our own pleasure, but to serve him, and most people are attempting to run away from him. (In congregations with members who like reading, Michael Green's book *Runaway World* [IVP] might be recommended, and copies should be made available on the church bookstall.)

Jonah is a prime example, as we heard in the Lesson/soundstrip. God told him to go and warn Nineveh to turn from their sins and he fled in the opposite direction.

Who was Jonah?

His existence and adventures with a whale are often regarded as mythical. Readers have to make up their own minds, but the case for the prophet being real should not be automatically written off. According to the Bible he lived at the time of Elijah and Elisha, when God was permitting quite a few miraculous events. Jonah is mentioned in 2 Kings 14:25.

Furthermore Jesus obviously spoke of him as an historical person. They both came from Galilee and when people were asking Jesus for evidence that he was the promised Messiah he referred them to Jonah (Matthew 12:40–41). Concerning the fish, the Bible makes no mention of a whale, but rather states that 'the Lord provided a great fish to swallow Jonah' (Jonah 1:17). Sperm whales are found in the Mediterranean Sea with large enough gullets to swallow a man and there is evidence that in 1927 a man was swallowed in this way and lived. On Jewish reckoning of days there is no need to believe Jonah would have been in the fish for more than thirty-six hours.

What Jonah came to learn, as we all must, is that it is absurd to think we can run away, or even swim away, from God and for three reasons (put up words as they are reached):

1. God knows

The terrible storm and the dice were evidence enough for Jonah, which was why he asked to be thrown overboard from the ship. Reference could be made to Psalm 139:1–7 and the Prodigal Son from the Bible. Other illustrations could include part of Francis Thompson's poem 'The Hound of Heaven':

> I fled Him down the nights and down the days
> I fled Him down the arches of the years:
> I fled Him down the labyrinthine ways
> of my own mind, and in the midst of tears
> I hid from Him, and under running laughter....

Eventually he stopped being foolish and gave in to the Hound of Heaven, God himself, and found true peace.

C.S. Lewis, author of the Narnia Books, describes his eventual capture by God in his book *Surprised by Joy* (Fontana, 1959 edn. pp 182–3): 'The Prodigal Son at least walked home on his own feet. But who can duly adore that Love which will open the high gates to a prodigal who is brought in kicking, struggling, resentful, and darting his eyes in every direction for a chance of escape?' God knows all about each one of us. Could any of us be so silly as to think we can attempt to escape from him? Besides:

2. God cares

Jonah knew because of the way the dice fell and the provision of the big fish. But you and I have far more reason to know. Jesus obviously saw there were parallels in his life with Jonah's:

Jonah	*Jesus*
Offered to die for sailors	Died for all sinners in the world
Three days in fish	Three days in tomb
Comes out alive	Resurrected from the tomb
Sent to pagans in Nineveh	Sent disciples into all the world

The supreme evidence that God cares was the cross (put up), which is where Jesus' life differed fundamentally from Jonah's. Whereas Jonah fled from doing God's will, Jesus wrestled in the Garden of Gethsemane and did it, because he cared. However:

3. *God forgives*

God did not want either a disobedient or a dead Jonah, but a repentant one. He wanted Jonah to be sorry for running away from him. The storm and fish were not meant for punishment, as Jonah was to come to see, but to bring him to repentance (a change of mind), so that God could forgive him and send him to preach to the pagans in Nineveh. Refer to 2 Peter 3:9 and 1 John 1:9. It is because God knows and cares about us that sometimes disciplinary events happen to us. God wants us to repent and believe that we might discover the joy of forgiveness, the satisfaction of serving him and the prospect of heaven.

Perhaps end by quoting the song from *Come Together* by Jimmy and Carol Owens: 'God forgave my sin in Jesus' name', stressing the line 'go in my name and because you believe, others will know that I live'. The song could then be sung by the whole congregation.

Michael Botting
Editor

75 Jonah (2) Discovering the Love of God

TEXT

Jonah 3—4; John 3:16.

AIM

To teach about the love of God.

PREPARATION

Prepare a soundstrip as described in the preparation to Talk 74, which can be used in place of the Lesson. Using either an OHP or Teazlegraph board make the following pictures:

1. A very respectable man and a tramp
2. A face with a black blob over the forehead
3. A conventional heart-shape with a black blob in the centre
4. The words: 'Jonah was prejudiced in mind'
5. The words: 'Jonah was selfish in heart'

PRESENTATION

Ask whether we behave any differently towards people who come to church if they have a different colour skin to us or are dressed markedly differently. Possibly tell the true story of a preacher who went to a very respectable church with a friend dressed like a tramp. (Show picture 1.)

The 'tramp' was shown to a back seat in a side aisle. When the preacher began his sermon with a similar question to the one in the above paragraph, there was considerable embarrassment when the 'tramp' was asked to come forward!

Remind the congregation of the story so far of Jonah the Jew, assuming that Talk 74 has been given recently. He was told by God to preach to nasty Ninevites, who after all were not Jews and were terribly wicked. Jonah fled to Spain, was involved in a storm, and with a fish, and given a second chance to obey God's command. Jonah had two problems, which could also be ours:

Jonah was prejudiced in mind (Pictures 2 and 4)

How could Jonah preach to Ninevites, who might repent and be forgiven by God? Heaven should be reserved for Jews only. We criticise prejudice in places like Northern Ireland and South Africa, but what about ourselves? Do we think that God really prefers whites or blacks like us? That he prefers the Prayer Book to the Alternative Services and older people to younger ones? Add other illustrations that are appropriate to your congregation.

Jonah was selfish in heart (Pictures 3 and 5)

The Ninevites repented, yet Jonah was very unhappy—how could God forgive such wicked, nasty people?

Explain the story of the plant. Ask who made it grow. Who let it die? Why was Jonah really sorry about it? Because he was selfish and wanted its shade. God expects us to tell people sin is wrong, but that through Jesus God can forgive. When people say that non-Christians have their own religions and should be left alone, it shows how little they know about other religions. God loves the world and sent Jesus to die for us all (John 3:16). So we must love everyone, too, and share God's message with them.

Michael Botting
Editor

76 Mary's Sword

TEXT

Luke 2:35.

AIM

To show that Mary, although the mother of the Son of God, was allowed the privilege of spiritual choice and obedience in common with the rest of mankind.

PREPARATION

Draw pictures as follows either on large sheets of paper, with some on small pieces, or on acetates for an overhead projector: (1) Figure of Mary and (2) baby Jesus, separately. (3) Joseph holding bird cage with two pigeons. (4) Temple interior and Simeon with arms outstretched. (5) A sword in the shape of a cross, to put over Mary's head. (6) Adult Jesus with (7) small crowd. (8) Two figures carrying body of Christ with background of crosses. (9) Background picture—top of hill with cloud. (10) Disciples with tongues of fire on their heads.

Headings are long but can be prepared for display if required. This could easily be made into a series of three talks (1, 2, 3; 4, 5; 6, 7, 8).

PRESENTATION

1. *Mary carried Jesus in her womb* (omit paragraph if deemed desirable)

   For nine months she (1) was joyous and full of praise to God: 'My soul doth magnify the Lord' (Luke 1:46).

2. *Mary carried Jesus in her arms* (2)

   She was joyous and obedient to God's will and God's word. She called him Jesus and took him to the temple with two pigeons (3, 4) (Luke 2:22–24).

3. *Mary saw Jesus carried by Simeon* (move baby (2) into Simeon's arms)

   This was *the first separation.*

   From Simeon: Words of wonder   —'Jesus Saviour to all'
   Words of Warning —'Jesus   Swordbearer
   to her'

   Jesus said later (Matthew 10:34) 'I came to bring a sword (into families)'.
   Don't be surprised if members of your family are unpleasant to you for being a follower of Jesus. A sword will pierce through your soul (put sword (5) above Mary).

4. *Mary saw Jesus* (6) *carried away from her by the crowds* (7)

   The second separation. Sharing him with others—we too have to let go of our children (who are really his) so we must not be possessive or resentful. Bring sword (5) lower down on to Mary.

5. *Mary saw Jesus carried away from her by his own teaching* (same picture)

   'Who is my mother?' he asked (Matthew 12:48) when she came to speak to him. 'She who does the will of my Father in heaven.' (*The third separation.*) The sword was digging deeper—not into the body but the soul. The sword was the word of God, the word of Christ, which divides soul and body, spiritual from natural (Hebrews 4:12). The sword separated Mary the natural mother of Jesus from Mary the spiritual disciple of Christ. The sword helped her to see her true position as an ordinary disciple or follower of Jesus.

6. *Mary was told that Jesus was carried by Joseph to the tomb* (8)

   The final separation of death. She was there at the cross and the sword went right into her (move sword (5) into Mary (1)).

7. *Mary saw Jesus alive and carried up by a cloud* (9)

   She saw him go, in all probability, and perhaps the sword went too (move sword (5) away). She was now accepted as one of the disciples and waited with them for Pentecost (Acts 1:14).

8. *Mary was filled with the Spirit of Jesus, and carried him in her heart for ever* (10) (Acts 2:4)

   'My soul doth magnify the Lord.'

Peter Barton
Malmesbury

77   The Lawyer and a Day of Questions

TEXT

Luke 10:25–37 (GNB).

AIM

To apply the teaching of Jesus in the parable by using the questions that surround the story.

PREPARATION

You will need an OHP and one acetate sheet with a large question mark filling the sheet in a light colour. On five separate overlays (I used one acetate sheet cut into five strips and attached to the frame) write the five questions: *'What must I do to receive eternal life?'*; *'What do the Scriptures say? How do you interpret them?'*; *'Who is my neighbour?'* and *'In your opinion, which of these three acted like a neighbour?'*; on the fifth overlay write *'You go then and do the same!'* (I also illustrated each question using the cartoon figures in the style of Scripture Union's 'Keynotes'.) You will also need two glasses of water and a bottle of food colouring or ink.

Begin by asking if there are any budding scientists in the congregation who would like to help you with an experiment. Ask for two volunteers; one to add one drop of colouring to one glass and the other to add twelve drops. Ask the congregation to notice the difference.

Say that the experiment might make us think about the way in which we help other people. Some of us are like the first glass; we pass out good deeds one drop at a time thinking that we've done our bit. Others are like the second glass and do a dozen things to help someone in need. The difference is obvious. God calls us to be generous in our helping of others, and Jesus once told a story about this.

READING: Luke 10:25–37

Displaying the visual with the question mark, explain that the parable of the Good Samaritan is probably the best-known and yet most mis-used story in the Bible. The questions surrounding the story will help us to understand the true meaning.

1. *Question 1 (v 25)*

   The lawyer asked this first question deliberately to test Jesus. It was a question that people were asking in Jesus' day (cf Luke 18:18) and a question that people are still asking today. Jesus deliberately didn't answer.

2. *Questions 2 and 3 (v 26)*

   Instead, Jesus asks the lawyer two parallel questions about his specialist subject. He gets the answers right (v 27) and Jesus commends him by telling him that he had in fact answered his own question (v 28). Most people today believe that by doing good deeds they will receive eternal life. Using Ephesians 2:8,9 explain that the Bible tells us that this is not so. By now the lawyer realised that he was cornered and that his answer was hypothetical because no one had kept, or could keep, the whole of the law. So to try and wriggle out of the trap he asks another question.

3. *Question 4 (v 29)*

Point out that the lawyer was also a Jew and was therefore under no obligation to love anyone who was a Gentile, and a Gentile certainly wasn't a neighbour! So, because Jesus knew that the lawyer was a Jew he thought Jesus would be on his side and let him off the hook by asking *'And who is my neighbour?'* Jesus replied with a parable that would have shocked him.

Retell the parable saying that the Priest in the story was rather like the gospel preacher on his way to a rally in order to preach about the love of God, who saw an old lady being mugged, but didn't stop to help because he was the first speaker and didn't want to be late! The Levite was rather like the average church-goer who thinks to himself 'I do plenty for the church...someone else can look after the tramps!' Draw the parallel with the first glass of water. Explain how the Samaritan went out of his way to help (cf the second glass of water) and this would have stunned the lawyer.

4. *Question 5 (v 36)*

The whole incident ends with a final question from Jesus. Recap as follows:

—The lawyer had asked Jesus about identifying a neighbour (v 24)
—Jesus asks him a question about being one (v 36)
—The answer was obvious (v 37a)
—The implication inescapable (v 37b) (Display last overlay)

Conclusion

Draw the parallels with the glasses of water and challenge the congregation about their generosity in kindness. Jesus told the story to show that *faith* (glass one) must be matched by *works* (glass two). The lawyer thought that what the Priest and Levite did was adequate (glass one), Jesus begged him to follow the example of the Samaritan (glass two). Jesus challenges us to do the same (point out that Ephesians 2:8,9 is followed by v 10). End by asking the congregation a question: *'How much colour are you prepared to put into someone else's life?'*

Bob Kiteley
Chester

78 Blind Bartimaeus

TEXT

Luke 18:35–43.

AIM

To tell the story of Blind Bartimaeus as an illustration of how we respond to the invitation to trust in Jesus by faith and not by sight.

PREPARATION

You will need an OHP and four acetate sheets prepared as illustrated with the words 'turned', 'trusted' and 'thanked' as overlays on visuals 2–4. You will also need a tray of three objects (I suggest a book, a map and an audio cassette) covered with a cloth, and a scarf for a blindfold.

PRESENTATION

Begin by asking the question, 'What must it be like to be blind?', and explain all that you couldn't see and do. Ask for a volunteer to be blindfolded and to guess what the three objects are on the tray.

While the volunteer is guessing explain that there are two kinds of blindness. Physical blindness when our eyes cannot

Visual 1

Visual 2

Visual 3

Visual 4

see, and inner blindness when for some reason a person is not able to perceive things as they really are, eg, lovers can be blind to each other's faults, etc. The Bible uses this second kind of blindness to express the fact that men and women are blind to God's truth about who he is, what we are and the world in which we live. People *think* that they know the answers to the big questions of life: 'Who am I?', 'Why am I here?', 'Where am I going?' etc, but in the end we can only make guesses.

Return to your volunteer and ask if he's guessed the objects. Hopefully he will tell you that they are a book, map and cassette. Then tell him that what you really want to know is the title of the book, the place of the map and the contents of the cassette... without removing the blindfold!

Using the first visual go on to tell the story of Blind Bartimaeus, and that as Jesus approached Jericho the noise would have made him curious so that he wanted to know what was happening. Explain that when he was told it was Jesus of Nazareth he would probably have tuned-in to the conversations of passers-by talking of the miracles they had seen Jesus do and heard about.

1. *Bartimaeus* turned *to Jesus*

   (Display visual 2 without the word 'turned' showing.) As the noise grew louder, Bartimaeus shouted in great expectation 'Jesus, Son of David, have mercy on me!' Ask the congregation if Bartimaeus saw Jesus. Ask them how he knew that it was Jesus if he hadn't seen him, and why he believed that it was in fact Jesus standing in front of him. Explain that others had told him and therefore Bartimaeus *turned* to Jesus in faith.

2. *Bartimaeus* trusted *Jesus*

   (Display visual 3 without the word 'trusted' showing.) Jesus stopped and asked for Bartimaeus to be brought to him and asked him a question (v 41a). Then came the cry of faith (v 41b).

Return to your patient volunteer! Remove the blindfold and explain that he now knows what Bartimaeus must have felt like, and show him what the objects are.

Returning to the story tell how Bartimaeus must have *trusted* Jesus to heal him of his blindness, and that Jesus' reply in verse 42 really means 'your faith has saved you' (AV). Go on to explain that Bartimaeus was healed of both physical and inner (or spiritual) blindness.

3. *Bartimaeus* thanked *Jesus*

Using visual 4 tell how Bartimaeus *thanked* Jesus in two ways; with his lips he 'gave thanks to God' and with his life he 'followed Jesus' (v 43).

Conclusion

In asking what we can learn from the story, explain that the second kind of blindness is far worse than the first. The Bible tells us that Satan is the one who ties 'blindfolds' around the 'spiritual eyes' of men and women (2 Corinthians 4:3–4, GNB) to prevent them from seeing who Jesus really is. Just as the volunteer could only make guesses as to what was in front of him, so, too, men and women can only make guesses at the truth of God. But they will know the real truth if they allow Jesus to remove the 'blindfold' from their 'spiritual eyes' (John 8:32, 44). Challenge the congregation by asking them if they have allowed Jesus to remove the 'blindfold' from their 'spiritual eyes', and that we must respond to Jesus in just the same way that Bartimaeus did.

Conclude by saying 'In Germany there is a bowl that is shaped like a drinking fountain and written on the bowl is the invitation to drink. But there is no water or tap in sight. However, if you stoop to drink "in faith", your head breaks an electronic beam, and fresh sparkling water begins to flow.'

(From David Watson *Is anyone there?* [Hodder], p 100.) That's a perfect example of faith.

Bob Kiteley
Chester

79 Zacchaeus

TEXT

Luke 19:1–10.

AIM

To show the difference Jesus makes when he takes control of a life.

PREPARATION

Obtain large-size boxes of (1) Quality Street, (2) Good News and (3) Contrast chocolates. Inside each box put a large sheet of folded paper with the words: (1) A chief tax-collector and rich; (2) I must stay at your house today; (3) I give to the poor.

PRESENTATION

Introduction

When we first meet Zacchaeus he is a hated and lonely man; and yet when we last see him, he is a liked and happy man. The story of his life is rather like the names of three well-known boxes of chocolates.

1. Quality Street

This very much describes the life of Zacchaeus before he met Jesus. We don't know the name of the street in Jericho in which he lived, but if we go by the sort of life he lived then it might well have been called 'Quality Street'.

Turn to Luke 19:2. What sort of life did he live? He was a tax-collector and rich. (Get the help of a child to open the first box and hold up the wording.)

Zacchaeus had a good job, but with CTC after his name he was a hated man. (Explain what a chief tax-collector was.) One of the Jewish books, the Talmud, went so far as to say that you could lie to three men — a murderer, a thief and a tax-collector! We know that Zacchaeus was rich, but much of his money had been gained unlawfully. He must have been a hard-hearted and selfish man.

So although he came from Quality Street, and had a beautiful house and a good job that brought in much money, he was hated and lonely and sad.

2. Good News

How lost Zacchaeus must have felt, for he was even prepared to climb up a tree on the chance of seeing Jesus, of whom he had heard so much. But how worthwhile that climb was! As he was there he heard the Good News which revolutionised his whole life. As Jesus was passing through Jericho for the last time, he stopped right under that tree.

What was the good news? Look at verse 5. (Get the help of a child to open the second box and hold up the wording.) 'I must stay at your house today.' What wonderful news for him! At last someone wanted to know him and be his friend. I wish I had been there. Imagine the Queen going down Oxford Street (name your local High Street) in a Rolls and one of the chief policemen climbs a lamp post to get a better view, and then suddenly the car stops!

Think with me of those words of Jesus: 'Zacchaeus, make

haste and come down, for I must stay at your house today.'
Notice two things:

(a) Jesus knew him. 'Zacchaeus!' he called. The same is
true of each one of us today. Jesus knows us: he knows
us through and through. And he wants to be our friend.
There is a chorus which says, 'The perfect friend's the
one who knows the worst about you, and loves you just
the same' (SU 297).

(b) Jesus commanded him. 'Come down.' No ordinary
person would dare command the chief tax-collector,
but Jesus did. He didn't say, 'Can I come to stay in
your house?' but 'I must come.' Sometimes we forget
the importance of Jesus and of his commands. The
most important command he ever gives is when he
says, 'Let me come in and take control of your life.'

3. *Contrast*

We will never know exactly what went on in Zacchaeus'
house, but it must have been a very wonderful encounter,
and a very thoughtful one too, because when he next spoke
in public, he said certain things which showed what a
change had taken place in his life. The change was as great
as the name of our third box of chocolates implies. Can you
guess the name? (Show third box and get a child to take out
the third sheet of paper.)

Turn to verse 8. Not 'I get' but 'I give'; no longer 'I rob'
but 'I restore'. What a contrast.

Whenever Jesus comes to take control of someone's life, a
contrast will be seen. Sometimes the contrast will be as
great as it was for Zacchaeus; at other times it will not be so
obvious to those who are looking on; but always the contrast will be there, because when Jesus takes control he
begins to run our life as he knows is best—best not only for
us, but best also for his perfect plans.

Summary

He came from *Quality Street* but was lonely and lost.

He heard the *Good News* and let Jesus in.

What a *Contrast*, as Zacchaeus started living and caring for others rather than for himself.

Garry Guinness
Worthing

80   Paul and the Philippian Jailer

TEXT

Acts 16:16–34.

AIM

To tell the story and to teach the truth of the words, 'Believe on the Lord Jesus Christ and you shall be saved' (Acts 16:31).

PREPARATION

The visual aid consists of four pieces of cardboard on to which are printed the headlines of the story: 'Paul put in prison', 'Feet fastened at Philippi', 'Doors dashed down', and 'Keeper converted to Christ'. It can be made by obtaining advertisements from the display rack of the local newsagent who will probably let you have them once they are out of date. Cut off the newspaper headings from the rest of the advertisement and stick it on to the top of the piece of cardboard. The words of the headlines can be written on with felt pen or made up from the newsprint of the advertisements. On the back of the cards write the words 'Today's', 'real', 'everlasting' and 'news', and the text, in such a way that when the cards are held up in a line and turned to reveal the text it can be read by the congregation. As the story proceeds, ask children to come up and display the headlines by holding them up to everyone. At

the end the cards are turned round by the four children to reveal the text. The headlines relate to the stages of the story in Acts 16.

PRESENTATION

Contrast the bad news of today's newspapers with the good news of Jesus. Tell the story relating it to each headline. Thus the first child comes forward with the headline 'Paul put in prison' and you then tell how this happened. Continue with each of the other cards in the same manner. For the fourth one, say that Paul told the jailer some good news. This was first of all that the prisoners had not tried to run away but were still there. This was good news to the jailer because it meant he would keep his job. But Paul told the jailer even better news: the good news about the God who had released them from the stocks. Get the children to turn their cards round at this stage to reveal the words 'Believe on the Lord

Jesus Christ and you shall be saved.' Show how the keeper did believe with his household, and rejoiced. Explain that this related to being saved from the power of sin. You could compare the release of the two prisoners from the stocks and the prison by the power of God to the release which God in power gives us from the bondage of sin through belief in Christ. Make use of the words 'everlasting news' to emphasise that this faith means 'everlasting life'.

Christopher Porteous
Beckenham

Biblical Index

315

Subject Index

317